WORKBOOK PRESS LLC
187 E Warm Springs Rd,
Suite B285 Las Vegas NV 89119 USA

Website: https://workbookpress.com/
Hotline: 1-888-818-4856
Email: admin@workbookpress.com

Ordering Information:

Quantity sales. Special discounts are available on quantity purchases by corporations, associations, and others. For details, contact the publisher at the address above.

Library of Congress Control Number:

ISBN-13:   978-1-963718-87-4   Paperback Version
               978-1-963718-89-8   Digital Version
               978-1-963718-90-4   Hardback Version

REV. DATE: 11/15/2024

HONG CHENG

Memoirs of a Turbulent Life through Rose-Tinted Dust Storm

Pu-Chin Hsueh Waide

CONTENTS

PROLOGUE

When I arrived, Baba was already settled at home. He did not want to be on life support anymore in the hospital and wanted to come home. So, my stepbrother arranged for a couple of hospice helpers, a hospital bed, and everything that was necessary to make his last days comfortable.

"Baba," I called to him softly when I entered the room, trying to hold back my tears.

"Ah, Chin'er [the name my parents used for me ever since I could remember], you have come."

The familiar smile crossed his face, and even the usual twinkle in his eyes shone through his decline.

"Yes." I breathed and smiled back. He reached for my hands and kept smiling. Behind me, I felt the soft arms of my sister, who had arrived a couple of days earlier, over my shoulder. I dared not catch her eyes. I did not want our father to see how sad we were. He always had a wicked grin when things got difficult and taught me how not to take life too seriously. It was he who taught me how to sing and dance and laugh at myself, and, most of all, not to take myself too seriously. I stood over him, holding his hands, and let his life flash by frame after frame. Then he finally let go of my hands and went back to sleep.

During those final days, four inexplicable, almost miraculous events happened, which I never will and do not want to forget:

First, that evening, after my arrival, my sister, stepbrother, stepmother, and I, were in the kitchen, while around the corner, down a small flight of steep polished granite steps, was my father's room. We were discussing whether to tell my cousin brother, TaTung, who had, for several years, been estranged, from my stepmother and her family, that Baba was dying. TaTung, had grown up with us in India, and he had almost considered our parents to be his own. My sister and stepbrother decided not to; then at that very moment, we heard shuffles of my father's footsteps coming up those rather dangerous steps. All four of us jumped off our chairs and looked around the corner to tell Baba not to come up those steps, but all we saw, was that he was sleeping quietly in his very high hospital bed. It would have been physically impossible for him to get off it. We looked at one another and returned to the kitchen, and I said, "See, Baba is cross. We must tell TaTung."

The others looked at me and nodded. "Tomorrow."

Second, I used to sit on the floor at the foot of Baba's bed and meditate every morning; and every morning I saw huge dark gray billowing clouds overhead. Then I became aware of a lot of confusion in the room next door and heard my stepsister answer the phone and lamenting in a loud voice, "My father is dying. I cannot give you directions as to how to get here. Find it yourself." She crashed the phone down.

My cousin, even though we had not yet told him, had also arrived at everyone's consternation and surprise.

Third, I used to sing my parents favorite WWII song, "He re juin zailai?" (When will friends meet again? But I could never remember the third line of the first verse, anyway, I began to sing to BaBa. As usual, when I came to that dreaded line, I messed up. Baba opened his eyes, shook his head slightly from side to side, and croaked that line to me, then he closed his eyes, and I continued and finished the son. Perhaps I was never intented to remember that line, it had been saved for this very moment.

Fourth, as I continued my meditation, I heard the doorbell ring. Someone went to open the door. "Ma'am, is there a Pu-Chin Waide here?" Whoever had opened the door must have nodded. "I've been driving around for an hour looking for this address, and these flowers are for her." They were from my friend, Hal Miller, in Virginia. At that very moment, the sky in my meditation totally cleared to be replaced by that "brilliant white light" I had read about when people were near death. *Am I dying too?* I thought to myself.

Then I realized: "Come, come, come, Baba is dying," I called.

Everyone rushed into the room, crying, wailing, and sobbing. He did indeed take his last breath while I continued to meditate. I did not weep at all. As I sat there in the white light, I saw in the far distance a tiny figure beckoning to me.

"Come," it said. As I drew nearer, I saw that it was my father. He was taking me to Dawu, his village on the border of Tibet and China.

"Lai, lai, lai," he seemed to mouth.

I have died too, I thought to myself.

PART I

HONG-CHENG: TURBULENT LIFE THROUGH ROSE-TINTED DUST STORM

Chapter 1

EARLY YEARS

The quiet, sleepy little village of Dawu at the border of China and Tibet was about to be awakened by the birth of their new citizen. A little Han baby boy was about to enter the world with a loud and lusty cry. It was the year of the Rabbit, 1914. Dawu was situated at the base of the snow-capped sacred mountain Nyitso-la of the Himalayan Range. The village had only one dirt road and was flanked by sunbaked mud-brick houses. It did not snow often, so most of the houses had flat roofs on which many root vegetables lay drying in the sunny but cold and dry air, or colorful laundry flapping gaily in the breeze.

I was born in one of the larger mud-brick houses because my father, Hsueh KungSweng, was the governor of the westernmost region of China, the magistrate of the District, and the head of the border patrol platoon appointed by the Emperor. He was a stern and tall man and was just able to stand upright in his home. He was striding up and down the dirt road outside his house when, at last, he heard the cry of the baby. He rushed into the house, through the outer courtyard, where he conducted his business every day; under a low overhead lintel into the inner courtyard, which was the women's quarters; and into the bedroom where the birth took place. He was happy to see that I was a boy; the first child was a girl, now almost four years old. Now he felt complete: there will be someone to carry on the name. He acknowledged, with an almost imperceptible nod, his frail but beautiful wife, who had a complexion like the finest porcelain and an oval face with a very high forehead and crowned with shiny jet-black hair, sleeked down by yak butter. She looked up at her strong husband, smiled, and gently handed me to him. He hesitated for a moment and took a deep breath as if to steel himself against such a tiny delicate, fragile human. "Don't be afraid," she said. "You have very gentle hands, and you will not harm him." Hsueh KungSweng very carefully took me into his arms and said, "Aya, little boy, I will call you ChiPei. Chi, you are the sixth generation out of the seven characters Hsieng Fen Huang Di (Emperor) had given to our family. Mine is Kung. Now it is up to you to pass the last character to your own firstborn." Six generations ago, in the times of Hsieng Fen Huang Di, there was a particularly fierce warlord who rampaged the countryside, looting and killing people. When this *tu-fei* (bandit) approached our ancestor's province, the then-governor rode out of the city gates to "welcome" the tufei. As soon as he was within reach, Hsueh galloped out to meet him, his long sword unsheathed and raised above his head as he clashed against the warlord, who was taken by surprise, as no one had dared to even come near him so far. With one stroke of his sword, Hsueh cut off the warlord's head and stuck it on a tall pole in front of the north and main gate of the city for all to see. News of this action soon reached the ears of the Emperor, who sent for Hsueh to the palace. "You have performed a great deed today and probably saved many the lives and properties of many families."

"Bieh Xia [Your Highness]," Hsueh said with his forehead pressed on the ground in front of the Emperor, "I was not afraid of that bandit. I did not want him to destroy my own village also, so I decided to get him before he had a chance to even step into my territory."

"And for such cleverness and bravery, I bequeath the tract of land in the region of Khanding to you and your descendants. I also give you the seven characters to the firstborn sons of your next seven generations."

Hsueh bowed his head seven times on the ground and stayed down until the Emperor exited from the public Assembly Hall.

Baba wanted to take his baby boy out to show the neighbors who had gathered outside the house to hear the news, but it was the first month of the lunar year—much too cold to expose a newborn. He put the baby back into the mother's arms, beamed speechlessly, and strode out to give the news. "We have a baby boy, and he shall be called ChiPei." The villagers cheered, and shouted, "Gong-xi" several times then went home. The children ran and skipped around, shouted, and sang. It was a good day.

Hsueh Taitai (Madam) then handed me to the nanny and went to the Kwang Yin Pusa's shrine, which was installed in a corner of the inner porch surrounding the inner courtyard in our house. She was a devotee of Kwang-Yin Pusa and had been praying for over a year for a baby boy.

Now the prayers had been answered, so she must give obeisance and thanks to the goddess. She gathered some fresh fruits, a few homemade cakes, two bowls of yak butter, and some incense to the altar. She could only walk very slowly on the crude stone floors because her feet had been bound since she was three, and the pain has been with her ever since, and will probably last through her entire life. After a few steps, her maidservant girl came to assist her to the shrine. A thick, soft cushion was already placed in front of Kwang-Yin for her to kneel on. Very slowly, her maid helped her down on her knees. Slowly, she kowtowed three times, each time gently touching the stone floor with her forehead; and then, she was helped up to a waiting upright chair. Breathing softly, she repeated "O me to fu" many times and was helped back to her bedroom and me.

Meanwhile, friends, neighbors, and well-wishers had gathered outside the house, craning their necks to try to glimpse the newborn. Suddenly, there was a loud shouting at the main door. The favorite neighbor across the street had brought the family "long life" noodles, Tibetan fried pancakes, and other sweetmeats and was demanding to see the baby boy. Tshering Doma tripped on the hem of her *boku* and almost fell across the threshold, in her haste to get to Hsueh TaiTai. She was a very friendly, short, and rather rotund Tibetan woman in her late twenties. Her rosy cheeks virtually glowed and preceded her like a beacon. She wore the typical apron in front of her boku to denote that she was a married woman.

"Aya, Hsueh TaiTai, gong-xi, gong-xi, a son, what good fortune"; and breathing heavily, she continued, "And I have four girls, 'Kung ju sum' [I swear to God], they are all good girls, but a boy would have been nice. He could have helped my poor husband in the fields when he grew up."

"Tshering Doma," Hsueh TaiTai said softly, "girls can help in the fields too, and they also help you in the kitchen and in cleaning the house. Do you think a boy will do that?"

Tshering Doma grinned. "You are right, TaiTai, but come, eat some of these *tupa* [long-life noodles]. I made them especially for you and Hsueh Lao Ye."

Hsueh TaiTai took a bowl; it was indeed just what she needed. Sated, they sat and talked for a short while, but she was getting tired and sleepy. Tshering Doma took the baby in her arms and was delighted to see he had a head of dark brown curls, not a trait common among the Han people. She looked up at Hsueh TaiTai, raised her eyebrows, and smiled.

"Yes," said Hsueh TaiTai, "isn't he special? I have never seen hair curl like that. Maybe I prayed too hard to Kwang Yin Pusa, and this was her extra reward!"

"Hsueh TaiTai, you rest now. Here is little ChiPei, and I will tell the neighbors." By then, the new mother was almost asleep, so she quietly left. Tshering Doma was ready to burst to tell all the neighbors about the baby's curly hair.

I was also called the Fourth Small Brother, as I was the known current fourth generation of the Hsueh clan. All the servants of house called him Fourth Little Prince; his father being Third; his two uncles being Dage, the eldest; and number 2, the second brother. I was told that I grew up to be a gentle and graceful little boy and was a favorite of everyone, but I was not allowed to go out onto the street unless accompanied by DaJieh (elder sister) and a servant girl. I used to watch the older street urchins play a game called 'dalo'. In this game, three shiny brass coins were thrown onto the dirt road; and the boys, with a set number of small stones, would throw them, one at a time from a set distance, and tried to strike the coins. Even as a small boy of three or four, I wanted to throw those stones and shout "dalo" when I struck one, then I would claim one of those shiny coins as a prize. I was convinced that I would do so; alas, I was only allowed to watch from the threshold of our house. As I grew older, I was allowed to go further and further from the house but always accompanied by DaJieh and Damu, the young servant girl, who was only ten.

Damu's parents were Tibetans, who were simple vegetable farmers and often sold their produce to the family. Damu was the third of seven children and who often helped her parents when they took their vegetables to the market.

One day, when they came to house, Hsueh TaiTai saw the lovely rosy-cheeked little girl and asked her if she would like to come and play with her daughter.

"Little one, what is your name?"

"Damu," she replied shyly.

"I have a daughter slightly younger than you, and we call her YuMei. Would you like to come and play with her and be her companion?"

Damu looked up, and her face shone with delight, but she was too shy to say 'yes' immediately. "I will have to ask Mama." She replied.

"Of course, you must, but come and tell me if she will let you."

Little Damu ran all the way home, and panting, she shouted for her mother, "Amma, Amma, can I go, please, please, please?"

"Go where, Damu? Where do you want to go?"

"Hsueh TaiTai has asked me to go and play with her daughter and be her companion. Oh, please say yes. I have seen that little girl. She seems so sweet and pretty. Please say yes."

"You are a lucky girl. That is a very kind family, and Hsueh TaiTai is particularly gentle and kind. When do they want you to go?"

"I don't know. I just ran home as soon as she asked me. I did not even think to ask her that."

"You silly girl, go. Go to her and ask her."

Damu ran all the way back and breathlessly told Hsueh TaiTai, "Amma says I can. When do I start?"

Hsueh TaiTai smiled and said, "You can start tomorrow. You may sleep in the same room as my daughter and help her keep it tidy. We will take care of all your food and clothing." Damu rushed away again, this time collapsing on the front step. "Amma, Amma, she said tomorrow, Aya, tomorrow. What shall I do? What do I take with me?" She was so excited that she could hardly contain herself. She went to the room she shared with her three sisters. They all hugged one another and danced around their room.

Damu then looked in her little box where she kept her belongings. She had two pairs of pants, one cotton, one made of yak wool for the winter;

two long Tibetan long gowns, again one cotton and the other padded for the harsh winter months; three long-sleeved shirts; and a few pairs of wool socks her mother had knitted out of the hair she combed off their Lhasa Apso dogs. She had only one pair of shoes, which she was wearing and had been handed down to her when her elder sister had outgrown them. She hastily put these items into a sack and waved her family bye-bye and ran off as fast as she could to the Hsueh family. At their doorway, little YuMei was waiting for her. This was the happiest day of her life, as it was also for YuMei. They greeted each other shyly. YuMei then took Damu's hand and took her to "their room." Damu was amazed to find that she was going to sleep in the same room as her little mistress. YuMei sat her down on her bed and called for one of the older maidservants to prepare another bed at the foot of her own for Damu, who will be her companion and friend forever! They have been together for just over two years, and not a day passed when they were not seen together, and now there was a baby brother to share. YuMei shared everything with her just like a real sister. Her main job nowadays was to help me and to make sure that I did not leave the house alone. She herself did not trust those rough Khamba urchins, who were dirty, snotty, and wild. Little did she know that I secretly admired and envied those boys and their wild ways and often wished that I could go out and play with them.

Then one day, the time came when I was allowed to walk out of the house by himself; it was the Chinese New Year, and I had reached the magic age of seven. Mma took out a white silk undershirt and black silk trousers, and a long royal blue silk-brocade gown. She called Damu to come and dress me, much to my dismay, as I could dress himself and did not want a servant girl to help me. After much argument and running around the house to keep Damu from catching me, I was finally allowed to dress myself. It turned out it was less easy than it appeared because there were many frog buttons on the shirt, which were difficult for my small fingers. At last, all was done, and I walked down the main street to the bakers to order the cakes and dumplings for the New Year celebrations. I stepped out with DaJie, unaccompanied by the servant girl. I was a sight to behold, all stiff and awkward in my brand-new outfit. Feeling self-conscious, I did not look up as I passed those street urchins who were visibly smirking behind their hands. I felt like a walking doll, and had not DaJieh been with him, I would have run home.

10

The dim-xin (snacks) maker was a "traveling seller" of yummy things. He went from village to village, house to house, during the numerous festivals, selling his ware; and all the children of the villages adored him. He could "morph" a simple lump of dough into the most mouth-watering, delectable morsel one could die for. His onion cakes, dripping with pork fat but so flaky and light, were enough to make the most roughened soldiers weep. The fillings in his dumpling were plump with delicious soupy meat, and his red-bean cakes made one think that these must be what the gods ate in heaven. In fact, this magical man was able to make an extremely good living by selling his wares just only during these few times a year. Like all the other children, my sister and I believed he was a magic man. We ordered our goodies and returned home. On the way, I wanted to visit the stables to see my favorite horse, which I named White Cloud because he was pure white with a silvery mane that hung down the left side of his broad and strong neck, but his real name was Old Dragon. He was the fastest horse in the village. I always had an apple or lump of brown sugar for White Cloud. I loved this horse and dreamed of the day when I would ride him during the annual races on Pao-Ma Shan (Race Horse Mountain) and bring home the silver trophy. But DaJieh told me that we had to get home as soon as the order was placed or Baba would be angry.

"I'll only be a short while. I have not seen White Cloud for a whole day, and I want to see him. You go home. I will come home very quickly."

"This is your first time out without Damu. Don't make Baba angry."

"Oh, all right, I'll be home soon."

The youngest syce (horse groom) was a friend and was very amused to see his Fourth Little Prince walk into the stables in all his New Year finery.

"Aya, look at you. Be careful. You will spoil your new clothes."

"I won't. I just came to see White Cloud."

Without my father's knowledge, I had become a proficient rider by the age of six. I could ride barebacked, standing up, facing backward. I was not afraid to mount any horse. I was like a monkey on a horse. But that day, when I entered the stables, I saw our large black pig in the outer courtyard of the stables, and thought, *If I can ride a horse, why not a pig?*

Without another thought, I jumped up on the pig, which was startled and leaped forward, squealed loudly, and began to run around the courtyard. Alas, the pig was exceedingly broad, so I could not get myshort legs around its belly; it was also very prickly and yet slippery to sit on, he began to slide down the broad backside of the beast. Finally, there was not the life-saving mane horses have to grab on to. Within a few minutes, I was on the ground; and as I fell, I heard a terrifying ripping sound of something tearing. I was covered with dust; my new black silk trousers had an enormous tear in the crotch, and my hair looked as if I had been caught in a dust storm. The young groom ran up and shouted, too frightened to laugh, "Fourth Prince, why did you have to go and ride that pig? Pigs are hard and slippery and without mane. If he did not throw, you are lucky."

"I need some glue quickly," I shouted.

"Whatever for? Anyway, from where I can get glue?" I was very puzzled.

"To glue my pants, of course." Then the groom realized and burst into laughter till tears ran down my face and my nose began to run too. I panicked and shouted, "It you do not get me glue, I will tell Baba that it was you who dared me to ride that pig." The groom suppressed a grin and promised to make some glue. He took some rice flour and mixed some water into it to make a thick paste. Glue. Soon all the grooms heard of the fiasco and came to help. They loved Little Fourth Prince and did not want me to get into trouble with Hsueh Lao Ye.

When I arrived home, the family was already seated at the round dinner table and waiting. I quickly took my place at the table and gingerly sat down on my stool, which was higher than everyone else's. Mma looked at me suspiciously and asked if I had had fun in the village. Jiehjieh gave a sly smile, which made me sick to my stomach as I was sure this mishap had been discovered. After dinner, I quickly rose and started to run to my room.

"Stop," said Mma. "Go and change your clothes before you go to bed. You are covered with dust. I can see that there is glue on your pants, so you must have torn it. If Baba finds out, you have been in some mischief, you will not only have curfew for many weeks, but he will also spank you with the PLANK! This is the New Year, so I will not blame you, only hope you have learned your lesson. So, clean up and get to your room before Baba asks for you."

I went to my room where Damu, trying to hide her smile, was waiting. I looked sternly at her and tried to act all grown up, suspecting that she already knew what had happened. The servants had their own means of communicating as fast as lightning. She helped me out of my uncomfortable New Year's garments and ran a bath in a small tin tub. The bath was soothing and comforting, and soonI was changed and ready for bed. Baba and Mma came in to say good night. I snuggled down into the quilt and pretended to be asleep; I did not want to look into my stern father's eyes, I was sure he could read what I was thinking about. But in truth, I was already asleep when Baba and Mma came into his room.

Their house had two courtyards, with roofed porches running the length of the inner circumferences. The main entrance with a high threshold, and a large double door located in the center of the outer wall. Rooms were arranged on either side of this door and around these porches. All the public rooms were around the outer courtyard; here, Magistrate Hsueh conducted his business or listened and managed the villagers' complaints. There were two "guestrooms" for out-of-town visitors and relatives on one side of the main doorway, and on the other side, there was a set of rooms for Hsueh's administrative secretary Tsung TseeYe Hsien-sen (Mr.) and his family. DaJieh and I were never allowed to "play" on this side of the house.

At the opposite end of this outer courtyard was a smaller "doorway" with a very low upper lintel and a very high threshold leading to the inner courtyard; thus, it was very difficult for anyone to rush in or out: one would either hit one's head on the low lintel or trip on the unusually high threshold—a clever deterrent for thieves and other "ne're-do-wells." This was the entrance to the "women's quarters," and around this courtyard were several rooms—on the right of the entrance a large master's bedroom for BaBa and Mma. My sister and I shared a room adjacent to that. To the left of the entrance, there were a few smaller rooms for the maids and men servants. Adjacent to the back wall of the courtyard was the kitchen, storage rooms, and bathrooms. There was a well in the center of the courtyard, with a small fruit-bearing apricot tree beside it. The fragrance of those flowers was always a source of great pleasure to Hsueh Taitai. In the southwest sunniest corner was a vegetable patch where the cook and his assistant grew cabbage, leeks, sweet peas, other green vegetables, and, of course, turnips, carrots, sweet potatoes, and few melons. The entire courtyard was paved with fieldstones, so it would be easier for the ladies with bound feet to walk. At the other corner of this courtyard near the far wall was a small door, which led to a fenced back compound where all the animals were kept. Here, a couple of goats, My pet sheep KalaKala and the infamous black pig in his own pen, and several chickens scratched about in the yard. These animals were not allowed into the inner courtyard, and it was the bane of little Damu's life to chase them out should they manage to wander in. It was also a playground for me. I loved to play kick the feathered shuttlecock or jackstones or chase little Damu around the well. When the apricot tree flowered, used to pull Mma to it to smell the flowers; then when the fruits set, I could never wait till there were fully ripe and would eat them raw and pay for them later with bad stomachaches. DaJieh and Damu were not sympathetic.

Outside the main entrance, there was a strong iron pole hammered into the ground, and on this stake was the family's fierce and much-loved Tibetan mastiff, or "lion dog." Most Tibetans had these working dogs. They were kept chained during the day but were off leash at night, But to the family, they could not be gentler and sweeter; a baby could take food out of its mouth without fear. I often rode on his soft back when I could hardly walk. Wanderers, who came too close to one of those remote dwellings at night were mauled and even killed by those faithful guardians.

A short distance from this family complex, were the stables where Hsueh LaoYe kept close to thirty horses. The syces (grooms) slept in the loft of the stables; here, they had their own cubicles, refectory, and washrooms. Hsueh LaoYe hired a cook to prepare all their meals, and a "groundsman" made sure that everything was swept and kept clean. He also made sure there was clean and fresh hay and grain for the horses and enough water for everyone. A special room was in one section of the stables where all the extra weapons and horse tackle were stored; otherwise, the groomsmen took care of their own weapons and kept them in their own cubicles.

Hsueh LaoYe's administrative secretary Tsung TseeYe Hsien-sen and his family lived in the left wing of the outer courtyard. The two families were very close and often celebrated the yearly festivities together. Since Hsueh Laoye was often out of town, he was comforted to know that Tsung Hsien-sen was around, not only to run the business but also to keep an eye on his family.

FunTse Lama

Mma was a very religious lady. In addition to praying at the Kwang Yin Pusa's shrine every day, several times a year, she also used to visit a holy man called FunTse Lama (Mad Monk). This lama lived in a cave halfway up the mountain ridge of KeDa LiangTse (Knotted Ridge) between the districts of Dawu and LuHo. I begged to go with her, but she always refused, saying that the mountain was too high and steep for a small boy.

"Then how do you go all that way, Mma, with your tiny bound feet?"

"Oh, I am carried all the way in a palanquin. I pay the bearers well, and they are happy to earn a few pieces of silver."

"I want to see this FunTse Lama, Mma. I want to see for myself if he is as mad as the boys in town say he is."

Finally, Mma agreed to let me go with TanZen, the household manager, not unlike an English butler. TanZen, also called Chiang KuanTse, traveled around the district Baba. He had been to LuHo, KanTse, and even as far afield as Khanding and Chengdu.

One day TanZen called me and said, "When I return from LuHe, I will be going right by KeDa LiangTse and thought my companions and I will visit the Fun-Tse Lama. Would you like to come with us? Hsueh TaiTai said that you are interested to meet this mad monk."

"Of course, I want to. I have been asking Mma to take me for a long time, but she kept telling me that the mountain was too steep and difficult for me. Ugh!"

"But you will have to meet us at the bottom of KeDa LiangTse. Can you do that? Will you be afraid? It is a long way from home, at least half a morning's ride."

"What do you mean afraid? You know how good a rider I am. I will come with Tempa if you are so worried." I was quite indignant.

"All right, I will see you a week from today at the base of KeDa LiangTse."

I was overjoyed and went to tell Mma.

"Oyo, son, you must be careful. That mountain is very steep and stony. One slip of your horse's hooves, and you are down the mountainside."

"Don't worry, Mma, I will be careful. If the path gets too steep, I will dismount and walk the horse. In any case, I do not like to stress him on such steep mountainsides."

On the arranged morning, I was excited and woke long before daybreak. I ran to the stables, but Tempa was already up and had saddled up White Cloud and a horse for himself. We took a couple of onion cakes and a flask of salty yak-butter tea for the journey. The sky was still dark but studded with its jewels, and the air was deliciously crisp and clear. We led our horses out and clipped-clopped through the quiet sleeping village. We did not exchange any words, as they were still not fully awake. White Cloud walked slowly through the village as if he knew he should not wake its people. As they rode, the sky lightened ever so gradually; and almost imperceptibly, the tips of Nyitso-La took on a pale-pink cast, gradually at first but then rapidly turned a deeper pink, then red, then bright orange, back to light orange, and finally blindingly white—the sun had risen. The snow glistened, and the grass, which was almost black in the night, took on its daytime color of jade green. "Tempa, I'm hungry. How long have we been riding?"

"Nearly two hours. Let us eat a *shapaleh* [onion cake] by that stream, and the horses can get a drink and some rest."

We walked over and sat down by the rushing stream. The water was so clear that had it not been rushing, one would never know that there was water in there. We ate the shapaleh and washed it down with mouthfuls of Tibetan tea, which was tea leaves boiled in yak milk and yak butter and a handful of salt thrown in. Unless one was used to this tea, one would never appreciate it. We washed our faces in the icy water, which thoroughly woke us up. There was a long stretch of relatively level ground ahead, and as we mounted, we looked at each other, without a word, the race was on. The wind rushed through my curly hair, and Tempa's rough Tibetan gown flew behind him.

"Choo, choo," and off we went. It was not long before While Cloud almost disappeared over the horizon. I stopped at the base of the hill and reined in to wait for Tempa, who pulled up shortly thereafter.

"Fourth Prince, your Old Dragon is too fast for my little pony. He is bound to win the race at Pao-Ma Shan."

"Yes, I know, if only Baba will let me ride him."

"Why would he not?"

"Because he says I am too young and some older nasty, aggressive kid may kick my horse in the belly and whip my face."

"Yes, Fourth Prince, it is true. Anything goes during that race. It is very corrupt and dangerous. But just think how wonderful it would be if you brought the trophy home. It will honor all of us."

"You know Baba. He will never give the trophy to me. He presents the prizes at the end, and he would never be seen, or even suspected, as favoring his own son, it was very sad to think that White Cloud would never win the trophy of being the fastest horse in town.

We continued to the next ridge and the one after that was the KeDa LiangTse. We then dismounted and waited for Tanzen and his friends to come. They ate the last shapaleh, drank the rest of the yak-butter tea, then lay down on the soft grass and fell fast asleep.

"Hey, you lazy rascals, asleep in the middle of the afternoon, eh? Get up, you," someone shouted. I jumped and was ready to fight, only to see it was TanZen and his companions.

"Hey, Tempa, wake up, you lazy donkey." TanZen kicked him gently in the side. Tempa also jumped up, arms ready for a fight.

"What's the matter with you young ones? So ready for a fight, eh? Ha-ha."

"Come, we must climb and get back down before it gets dark, or we will not be able to see anything."

"Aya, you scared us. I thought you were some *tufei*." It was steep for the horses, so we left them down below. Those horses were so bonded with us that they would never run away. The climb was tough, made more difficult because of the rubble; so, with every three steps up, one slid down one. Halfway up the hillside, they saw a cave, and standing at its mouth was a stark-naked man with arms akimbo, staring down at us. His long hair reached down to his waist, and his long straggly beard was matted with twigs and leaves all glued together with phlegm. He laughed heartily as we approached.

"It's him, Fun-Tse Lama," said one of TanZen's friends. "It's the Mad Monk." This man quickly took out a long white scarf, (*khada*) and presented it to FunTse Lama and bowed. FunTse Lama took the khada and wrapped it around his neck and chuckled. Then we offered him dried beef strips, tsampa (roasted barley), yak-butter, salt, and tea. Fun-Tse Lama, giggling, took all these offerings and said in Han Chinese, which surprised us,

"Hee-hee-ee, I have not had butter for a long time. Come, let's have tea." He was delighted and hopped about like a monkey, mumbling to himself, "Ooh, butter, it's been such a long time, hee-hee-hee." Then turning to Tanzen, "Go get some snow and put it in this kettle. I do not have yak's milk, so we will have to use water." The kettle he gave to TanZen was pitch-black. FunTse Lama piled some dried leaves and twigs on the ground; then he rubbed his hands and blew on the pile, which suddenly burst into flames. "Aha, good, good," he mumbled to himself again. "Hey, you snow collector, bring the kettle here and put it on this fire. When the water boils, I will put in the tea. When it boils again, I will add the butter, he-he—yes, butter—and last salt. It will be good. I haven't had butter for a long time." All the contents were poured into a

18

tall and fat bamboo culm and churned with a plunger for several minutes. Then FunTse Lama told us to bring our bowls, which he filled first before filling his own. Tibetans carried their own wooden bowls and cups with them when they traveled; sometimes these bowls were clad in silver and sometimes studded with turquoise and coral beads on the outside. We sat down on the stony path and settled with our steaming bowls of salty tea, when he looked up and noticed me. "You are young, Hsueh Chi Pei, are you not? Hei-hei, your father—he is too good a man, poor man, too good, too good. But you will go very far beyond these stars. Look at them now because where you go, you will not see these same ones." Then he began to cry, "You poor young thing, so much loss, so much, too much suffering, so much loss. Never mind, some great happiness too, yes, yes, happiness too." We drank our tea silently, not knowing what to say or do. I was very puzzled and did not know which way to turn. What did he mean by so much loss? What about not seeing the same stars? Then suddenly, FunTse Lama leaped up and started to shake the bowl he had cradled in his hand and, trembling, cried, "Ah tseh, ah tseh, ah tseh [poor things, poor things]." He rocked back and forth and continued to lament. Then he suddenly picked up a large stick and began to beat one of the men called Tung. Everyone got up and rushed down the mountain. When they reached the bottom of the mountain, Tung had registered neither bruising nor any pain, though at the time of the beating, it had hurt very much. Later, they understood that FunTse Lama had a premonition that Tung's family was in danger of the imminent earthquake, and he had wanted to drive him and everyone home as fast as possible. But at the time, no one understood what was going on in his head, only that he was an unpredictable madman. This lama was embodied with supernatural powers, which the ordinary folks did not understand, especially the true inner meanings of his words and, therefore, only treated them as the ravings of a madman. It was always amazing to the local people that he could live without a stitch of clothing in a snowbound land. His fluent Han Chinese could not be the ravings of a madman because it was obviously learned. His insight and his sensitivities were achieved through years of intense meditation such that he became completely in empathy with his surroundings. There were no differences between himself and his environment any longer.

I returned home and told Mma about the meeting with the Fun-Tse Lama.

"Why didn't TanZen ask him to explain instead of driving us away like that?"

Mma smiled and said, "There is an old Chinese saying, 'If you can know something three days before the event, you will become a millionaire.'"

"And all that talk about me going beyond these stars—what does that mean? And all that loss? What do I have to lose? What happiness? I am happy now." I was totally dumbfounded and at Mma, who turned away so that I would not see a tear drop down her cheeks. She understood because she had seen the signs too, and the greatest unhappiness and loss was her own.

In the early 1900s, there was a meeting of a number of famous monks and lamas at the Litang District: LungKa Lama, a Rinpoche (reincarnate lama known to Chairman Mao TseTung); two Chinese monks called Ta FaScee and Ta Kang FaScee from the Ba Ang District in Sichuan; plus, another Rinpoche named FuTu KePu; and numerous others. During this meeting, a naked man with wild hair and beard walked in, much to the astonishment and consternation of all the other dignitaries, except LungKa Lama, who immediately recognized him as the FunTse Lama. He at once offered the new arrival the golden-colored brocade robe and a red hat. FunTse Lama took them and kowtowed to LungKa Lama and said,

"Rinpoche, I am not accustomed to any kind of clothes and hat, especially such grand garments." He shook the robe and hat, and the whole outfit went up in flames. This action astonished and shocked the Chinese monks present, but they deeply respected this mad lama and realized that he was no common magician but a true Tibetan Buddhist lama. It was not magic nor illusion but genuine fire!

Unforgettable Earthquake

Hsueh LaoYeh's administrative secretary, Tsung TseeYe Hsien Sen and his family, lived in the right wing our house, and we often dined together. However, when LaoYeh was away, Aunty Tsung invited Mma, my sister and Lamu, our servant girl, to eat with them. One day as we were sitting down to dinner, there was a tremendously loud crack, like thunder, right over our house. The bowls and plates slid from one side of the table to the other, and even the furniture started to move across the room. In those areas, where superstition was the norm, the people thought that they were being attacked by evil spirits. Then we heard Lamu, who was born in this district and had experienced earthquakes before, scream, "Go outside. Go outside quickly. This is an earthquake." Mma took JiehJieh and my hands and rushed out, and just as Lamu came out, the ceiling of the living quarters came crashing down as did the main walls of the back compound. These walls were built to withstand earthquakes because they were shaped like skinny pyramids—wide at the base and narrow at the top—so during a quake, they would collapse rather than topple over, which can be more dangerous. Fortunately, the front section of the house was still standing. This happened three days after the Fun-Tse Lama experience. Tsung BeiBei ran in from the office to see what could be done. The kitchen was demolished, and the cook was crawling over the rubble, grumbling that his best copper and brass pots were all dented and dirtied. Just at that moment of disaster, he had been squatting on the lavatory, when in a flash, the four walls around him collapsed and he was totally exposed. All those who saw him were hysterical with laughter – such is the nature of the Khambas – they laugh at times of disaster. Tsung BeiBei comforted him by promising that he would take him to the market as soon as the quake stops, he said,

"Don't worry about a those. I will take you to the market and buy you a new set of pots and a new kettle."

Then he sent a messenger to BaBa to tell him of the disaster.

"Now we must be prepared because one earthquake is always followed by other smaller ones. Be careful of where you step in case the ground opens under you. We must find a place where we can spend the rest of the night." Mma proposed that they go to the KuanYin Pusa's temple, but when we got there, so had the rest of the village. Everyone was chanting, "O Me To-Fu."

Finally, we went to the new school BaBa had built:- a permanent wooden structure with a peaked roof and tables and stools and benches in the schoolrooms. Till then, the schools were held in tents with rugs strewn on the ground for the children to sit on. BaBa had told everyone that the new school would not be in a tent, that the walls would be permanent, they would be made of wood and mud-bricks. The ceiling would not be flat but would be shaped like a tent. This was the first formal elementary school, and being so new, many of the villagers were very suspicious and laughed at the wooden building. When it came to schooling time, they did not send their children to this school. Some of the parents went so far as to catch the street urchins or hired nomads and paid homeless beggars to attend. They considered the school fees as a form of taxation.

Tsung BeiBei took our family there and told Mma that the roof will not collapse because it was not flat and did not have vegetables, and such, stored on top to add to the weight. He also told her that he had sent a messenger to LaYeh who would be coming home soon. I, being ever curious, stood by the door and watched and observed everything. saw that the jailhouse wall had collapsed, and some of the criminals were rioting, looting and threatening the villagers. Tsung BeiBei called in the soldiers to protect the people from these ruthless bandits. One village elder, YienBow Tseng, father of ten, had sent his servant to look at the conditions of his home. I saw the ground suddenly cracked opened and that poor servant disappeared into it, then the ground closed again. When YienBow Tseng came to report about his poor servant, Mma took DaJieh and me into her arms and wept. Everyone was terrified. As I watched these events, I began to understand what FunTse Lama was trying to tell them in KeDa LiangTse Shan. Years later, I was finally able to appreciate the miracles and tales of that old Mad Monk. Also, I never got over my own fear of even the minutest tremors of the earth, even up to today.

Chapter 2

Primary And Secondary School

Baba called me to his office one morning, as usual, to teach me the Tang poems I loved so well, but instead of sitting on the stool at his place, BaBa showed me to an intricately carved high-backed chair. It was not a comfortable place for a small boy. It was far too deep, wide, and high; and my feet dangled down awkwardly.

"*Ertse* [son], when we moved to this larger and newer house, the work at my job has also increased, and I will have to travel even more. There is a new movement in the country where some people want to overthrow the Emperor. They do not want to be ruled by him and his courtiers and advisors. They want the common people to select their owner leaders, so there is more and more unrest around the country. I am one of the many officers appointed by the Emperor to protect our country, and since I am in charge of the southwest and western region of China, a very large tract of land, I must go around and see to the law and order of these places."

I tried to understand, but all I could see was that I shall not be learning any more Tang or Sung poems, I was very sad and softly whimpered, I could not let BaBa see that because, according to the Kong FuTse (Confucius) principle, only women wept.

"So, after many weeks of searching and deliberation, I have decided to send you to a well-known private tutor called Yu FuLo. This *hsien sen* [teacher] has a twelve-year-old nephew called SungPei and a thirteen-year-old daughter called BeiChow. Though SungPei is a Han Chinese name, it was later discovered that he was a Rinpoche, (reincarnated lama) and was, therefore, not allowed to continue with his Chinese studies and had to change to study Tibetan scriptures."

I nodded and was happy that I would not be the only student, and who knew, they might become my friends.

We started tuition the very next day. I went to Yu FuLo hsien sen's house, which was only a few houses from ours, and found that SungPei was already sitting on his stool at the large square table. There were sheets of squared pieces of paper in front of him, an inkstone and stick on his right, s small dish of water, and two brushes. I nodded, and the other boy responded, then sat down on another stool to his left. There was another taller stool opposite SungPei. We waited and waited. Finally, SungPei whispered, "FuLo LaoScee [old teacher] is always late. He moves very slowly and can hardly hear, so you will have to recite very loudly." Then a very old man, dressed in a long mandarin light-grey gown, appeared from behind a curtain. He had a long thin beard, which seemed to be an extension of his thin straggly gray hair.

"Hurmph, Aya, late, I am late again. Aya, why does everything seem to move so fast these days? Hurmph." Then noticing me sitting with SanPei, he said, "So you are Hsueh KungSweng's son, Chi Pei. Humm? How old are you?"

"I am six, LaoScee. I will be seven in the first month of the New Year."

"Hurmph. So, you want to learn Tang poems? Your father says you can already recite most of them. Are you that clever then?"

"No, LaoScee, I just like them. I also like the Sung dynasty poems." I knew, as soon as I said that, that was the wrong thing to do.

"Oh, that clever, eh? That clever? We will see how clever you really are. Now, the two of you, take your ink stick, put a few drops of water on the inkstone, and grind it gently on the stone." We did this for several minutes; then he said, "Take your small brush and dip it softly on the ink that has been produced on your stone, like this," and he showed us.

I already knew how to do that because BaBa had begun to teach me calligraphy as soon as I could hold a brush upright. SungPei also knew. He winked at me and did what he was told.

Then LaoScee said, "Pick up your brush, wrist straight, elbows off the table. Keep your brushes vertical. Do not rest your elbow on the table. Now lift the brush from the inkstone to your paper and write 1 ten times."

We did as we were told. He came over to the table and examined our writings.

"Hurmph, good, good, good. You boys know how to write 1 very nicely. Do you know that this is a very important letter in calligraphy? It can reveal your inner strength or weakness, eh, eh, eh? Did not know that, eh?" He chuckled.

We continued this, plus 2 and 3, for almost an hour, tour wrists were tired, and because we had to keep their elbows off the table at all times, ourr right arms began to feel heavy and achy. But most of all, both SungPei and I were bored. We stole looks at each other but carried on.

At last, he exclaimed, "Haola, haola [okay, okay], you may now rinse your brushes in the water bowl and put your brushes down." Then he suddenly shouted, "DO NOT PUT YOUR BRUSH VERTICALLY in the water bowl. You will break all the hairs, and I will spank you hard if you do!" We were shaken from our boredom. Obediently, we gently rinsed our brushes and rested them on the side of the inkstone. "You may go into the courtyard and do some breathing exercises." They went out, breathing sighs of relief. What a first day of school.

There we saw BeiChow, who was the eldest granddaughter of Yu LaoScee, playing "kick the feathered coin" game. She had to stop her schooling when she turned thirteen and had to help around the house: going to the market, cooking, cleaning the rooms, sweeping the courtyard, tending to the vegetable plot, and so forth. After the short "fresh air" break, we returned to the classroom to continue ourr lessons. Most of the time was taken up by learning how to write properly with our brushes. This went on from one day to the next. Yu LaoScee was too old to do any real teaching and often fell asleep at the table, and sometimes he did not even show up so that more and more often he sent his assistant to check on us. SanPei and I usually just chatted and played paper games and scribbled and drew on our little blackboards with chalk. The assistant did not care or do much. Class was usually dismissed at noon.

BaBa was very disappointed with the situation, and finally took him out of the "school" and sent me to one of his friends, Dr. Lan SaoRu, whom I called Lan BeiBei (Uncle Lan). Lan BeiBei was educated in France and had earned his MD degree there. It was customary for students to live with their tutors, and in exchange for the teaching, they had to do some household chores and help around the house. So, while I was a student of Lan BeiBei I lived with Him and his family. There was another older student living with him also, whom he addressed as 'older fellow student.' This young man was not there as a student. His work was to copy articles and literature of a kind I did not understand. For the first time, he came across two words—*tse hua*—among the pieces he had copied. He did not know what these meant, only that they had something to do with *red*. After dinner one evening, we had retired to our room, which I shared with "older fellow student.

I said to him, "You do not have to be so secretive anymore. I know what you are writing about. I know the meaning of those two characters, *tse hua*."

"What do they mean?" he challenged.

"They mean *beggar*," I replied proudly.

The older fellow student burst out into guffawing laughter and said, "Yes, yes. You are perfectly right. Now go to sleep. I must take you home tomorrow." I did not know that *tse hua* was the cryptic name for Communist. It was my first encounter with this organization. The 'old fellow student' was just about to take me home when my father, who knew what *tse hua* meant, had learned what had happened and had sent a servant to fetch me. BaBa being under the employ of the Emperor, naturally was not sympathetic to the Communists. Anyway, it was almost New Year, and the holidays were imminent, so I did not stay with Lan BeiBei. BaBa did not let me return after the holidays.

After the New Year festivities, BaBa took me to another private school. It was situated on a large compound of swept dirt, and there were three rooms kept especially for teaching. These were the classrooms. We went into one of them. Behind a large rectangular wooden table sat a very kindly elderly gentleman, with a straight back and piercing black eyes. BaBa took me up to him and said, "Kowtow to your venerable old teacher. You must listen well to his scholarship." I kowtowed to him three times, hitting my forehead on the ground each time. After seeing that this was correctly done, his father left. The old venerable laoscee (teacher) never took his eyes off his new stuent.

"What is your name, little boy? How old are you?"

"Hsueh ChiPei, I just turned seven after the New Year festivities."

"This is your classroom, and they are your classmates."

I looked around and surveyed the classroom. At the front end was a long table for the teacher, and directly in front of this was my small desk and chair. There were two other desks, at each of which sat a boy of about the same age; these were brothers. These two boys were watching me closely. Behind my desk was a door leading to another room with three oblong tables and three chairs. Two older boys were seated at two of the three tables but no one at the third table. Later, I learned that this table and chair belonged to Lao Da, the oldest student, but he already had a job in town and so could not attend school every day.

The first thing I had to learn was Tang poetry, which BaBa had already started to teach me. I liked them very much and was good at composing couplets in this style. I wished, even then, that I could be a poet all my life.

After the initial few days, teacher Lo, or Lo lao scee, announced, "Tonight you two Han brothers and ChiPei will come home with me for dinner. I have asked the school cook to prepare a special meal for my new students." In such a large *ya men* (official compound), he had the authority to order a specially prepared meal for his students. Lo hsien-sens health was poor; and unfortunately, six months after I entered his tutorship, he retired. Lo *Hsien-sen* was replaced by Mr. Tsang. Tsang Laoscee had succeeded my father in Dawu. Though he was a very honest and good man, he had no ability to govern. After an unhappy year at Dawu, he not only left government service but also changed his career to become a teacher. His fellow workers thought he was stupid to give up such a good and well-paid position, where one was provided with comfortable living quarters, which was very difficult to come by, in exchange for a poorly paid teaching job without living accommodations. However, Tsang *hsien-sen* was not deterred and turned out to be a good teacher who was devoted to his students. Unfortunately, he favored one of his students: the young stepmother of the Han brothers who did not appreciated the situation and was often rude and obstreperous. Early one morning I was woken up by his father, "Wake up. Go. Go to Tse UrPo Temple. Pay our respects to Lo *hsien-sen*. He is very ill."

Lo *hsien-sen* asked when I got there, "Where is your father?"

"Baba said to tell you that he is very sorry that he could not be here personally to see you because he had to go out of town," I said.

"Your father is one of the few government officials who is truly honest, and he is well respected by all the local people. Tell your mother what I said and not to worry about him." Then he looked at me intently and said, "You are not a genius, but you are not stupid either. If you studied well and with diligence and apply yourself, you may become someone of note!" I had no idea what he was talking about, and after a while, I said good-bye to him, "Lo *hsien-sen*, I must be going. See you again." But I never saw him again.

A few days later, BaBa took me to visit Mr. Hwa, their neighbor, and his younger brother ChungJuin. I was told him to address Hwa hsien-sen as Da Ke (Big Brother) and ChungJuin as Ke-ke. Both these boys were enrolled in the Khangding Primary School. BaBa told me that I was going to that school too. ChungJuin became my classmate and best friend for many years.

Khanding Primary School

Early next morning ChungJuin came to fetch me to go to school. This was the first time I was going to a public school; up till then, I had been tutored privately. The first thing that ChungJuin did was to take me to see the principal. I prepared to kowtow to him as he had been taught, but Principal said that it was unnecessary, a simple bow was sufficient. He was only to bow to all the other teachers individually, and to the student body in general. No more kowtows.

I was taken to the classroom where I saw many boys of my age. They all stared at me with curiosity because of my curly hair, of which he had not been aware until that day, and that hair had made him look different from everyone else. ChungJuin clapped and welcomed me to their class and then suddenly shouted, "Attention! Rise!"

Everyone stood up to attention as our class teacher, Hsien-Sen, walked into the classroom.

"Sit," ChungJuin shouted again, and everyone sat upright on the chairs. I did know where to sit.

"You there, you are new, sit in the back row." Hsien-sen pointing at me "second seat from the right."

ChungJuin was introduced as the prefect of the class and sat down beside me. That was the first day of school for a seven-year-old. I was glad to have met ChingJuin who guided me through school during those first days.

At the left of classroom was a veranda with three steps. To the right of these steps was a large hall called the Hall of the Three Immortals. The Middle Immortal had a very red face and a very long beard, almost down to his knees. This was General Kuang Kung, with whom I was already very familiar as there was a statue of him in Dawu. The Immortal to the left of Kuang Kung had a white face and a very long beard; he was General Yo Fe. The Immortal to the right of Yo Fe rode a tiger and held an iron whip in his right hand. I later learned that he was the god of wealth. I discovered that the school was named after those Three Immortals, but it was never very clear as why a god of wealth was ranked among those other two very revered generals who had fought in the Three Kingdoms Warring Period. Kuang Kung and Yo Fe were famous for their honesty and justice, so how does wealth come into this? I was puzzled and did not understand. Every spring and autumn, people came to pay respect and worship these "gods."

On one particular autumn festival, the principal announced that all students, including the seniors, who had been given the option not to, must attend the worship of the Immortals and were not to be late for the service. After the worship, the principal gave all the students and teachers a day off and told everyone to go home, but they were to be back by nine before the gates of the school were closed. However, some of my friends and I decided not to go home, giving the excuse that we had to practice our flutes for a school concert that we were performing later. We waited. At nine o'clock, the main gate was closed; then my friends and I stealthily climbed over the wall of the school and jumped onto the playground outside the compound. Just like smoke, they quickly sneaked down the hillside to a small restaurant to eat wonton. These tasted particularly good as all forbidden fruits did. When we came out of the little place, it had become much colder, and a strong wind had risen, which blew dirt up and around them. They ran up the hill as fast as they could toward their school, but halfway up, they had to pass a pagoda, a tall lighthouse-like building. This was a kind of incinerator where people came to burn effigies to appease the gods or ask a favor of them. These small pagodas were very common everywhere. Suddenly, we saw lights coming up the hill. They looked scary for little primary school kids, brave though they might be.

"Aya, Aya, oil lanterns. Must be the teachers. Quickly, hide. No, hurry up to the school. Quickly climb over the wall," so saying, the tallest and oldest boys, had no trouble, and over the wall they went. But two of my classmates and me were not so lucky. We crouched behind the pagoda and waited, hearts pounding like the drums the lamas beat in the monasteries, terrified, because coming up the hill was none other than the principal. We crept into the pagoda, and at the same moment, a particularly strong gust of wind blew up a swirl of dust, which accompanied us into the pagoda, giving us a ghostly image. The principal was frightened out of his wits, he ran up the hill toward the school's gate, panting and shrieking to the gatekeeper, "Hsiao-Hong, Hsiao-Hong, open the gate. Open the gate." As soon as it was opened, he rushed into the schoolyard in a great panic. We three then slowly crept out of our hiding place, climbed the wall, and returned to the dormitory. The other flutists came and softly asked, "Did the principal see you?"

I answered, "He was so terrified as he thought he had seen a ghost and rushed so nervously and quickly into the school that he did not have eyes for anything else."

Then with great glee, we embellished our escapade to our fellow delinquents school mates. But we were relieved that we had not been discovered. During the assembly that morning, Hsiao-Hong told us that the principal had met ghosts near the pagoda that night. He was now feverish and might have to stay in bed for several days. We truants suppressed a smile and did not tell the gatekeeper that we had "helped" the ghost that night by throwing sand at the principal. So, another teacher, Pen Hsien-sen, conducted the assembly instead.

Playing the Flute: Autumn Festival

The annual Autumn Festival was the paying of obeisance to Kong FuTse (Confucius). Written in very large characters in the assembly hall where the ceremony was held were the words "Former Pinnacle of Success—Kong FuTse." The original temple was in ruins because of the earthquake, so he was temporarily moved to our school because we had a large hall, which could accommodate many people; a stage; and a space enough to paste those characters beside Kuang Kong's face.

My friends and I were still playing card games and chess at three in the morning when we heard the whistle. What happened? They wondered and ran to the middle of the school hall to see Pen Hsien-sen who had called us to assemble. It was time to rehearse the concert they had been preparing for the celebration of Kong FuTse's birthday, but at three in the morning? Pen Hsien-sen said, "I called you so early because I wanted to make sure every student is here and also to test if you boys are really prepared!"

Most of the children were full of sleep and confusion. Anyway, they started their practice. At one side of the assembly hall was the accordion; in front of this stood the flutists among whom I was the leader in spite of being the youngest. On the other side, eight students held up long wild turkey feathers—a most impressive sight, even the Old Sage had said that such feathers should only be used to celebrate the Emperor's birthday, not commoners such as himself. Ah, well, he was not there to object. This went to prove that Kong FuTse's character and scholarship are "sky high." Fame and fortune did not impress him. We began to sing his song:

Sacred characters as high as the sky

Greatness of Kong FuTse, Thou art high,

Even though he is not emperor, he shares a common skin as him.

Here to save and teach us generation after generation.

Millions of generations.

Oddly enough, I later discovered that this tune was the same as the Japanese national anthem: the melody is serious and dignified. I did not know how our school had obtained this tune from Japan. (Even after eight decades, I still do not know).

During the Autumn Festival, it was customary for our school to participate in the parade through town. The drummers were in the front of the parade, then the flutists, followed by the Boy Scouts, the teachers, and, finally, the rest of the students who were dressed in their best tan-colored shirts, navy blue shorts, and white socks and shoes. Smart red scarves were tied around their necks, and on their heads, tanned cotton caps rested precariously on heads of short straight hair, except for me, which was curly. The principal of the girls' school led the parade. He was a very modern, intelligent, and considerate gentleman. He participated in all manner of social activities in the town. He wore a Boy Scout uniform, held a baton in his right hand, and blew a large whistle and shouted out the commands. The local people lined up on either side of the road and clapped and cheered as we passed. This encouraged the drummers to beat even louder and harder and the flutists to blow with even more vigor. We played student marches over and over:

Hold up my elder brother's 'han-ji' as a flag,

Little brother rides a wooden horse;

All the neighboring brothers bring your guns,

Let us go to the mountains and become soldiers;

In the mountains, the bugles are sounding,

Mountain people come out to look,

Mountain people do not be alarmed,

We are not foreign soldiers, nor are we bandits,

We are only students pretending to be soldiers;

In the future we will fight the foreigners,

We will protect our property and our four billion people.

This was the patriotic song we sang because the Chin dynasty had been put down only fourteen years ago, and the people in the border areas were still afraid of skirmishes. After the parade, they were all allowed to go home for the holidays.

Next morning, as soon as breakfast was over, BaBa told me to accompany him to the Hwa family. When we arrived, Big Brother was doing his morning exercises in the courtyard; but when he saw us, he stopped and came in to greet us.

"Hsueh BeiBei, how are you? Please come in and take a seat."

I saw ChungJuin outside, watering the plants, and I was just about to go out to join him when BaBa admonished me and told me to stop. He looked very stern and ordered me to give my flute to Big Brother Hwa and said, "I sent ChiPei to school to learn books, not to play flutes. I saw him yesterday at the parade, looking so spirited, blowing that flute, I felt ashamed. So, I am now returning the flute to you. Please tell the principal that I do not want my son to learn how to play the flute or the drums, and if it continues, I will remove him from the school."

DaKe (Big Brother) Hwa's smile flashed weakly across his face, but it was wiped off immediately because BaBa was extremely serious and his countenance was very stern. ChungJuin came in from outside, for he had heard what my father had said, and bravely addressed him, "Uncle Hsueh, his position as leader of the flute section was chosen by all of us fellow classmates. He is the best among us, and we admire him greatly and felt honored that he had accepted our vote of confidence. Please, Hsueh BeiBei, don't return the flute. We need him."

BaBa stood firm, his voice sounded as if cutting a nail, he said, "This cannot be. He must return the flute. I do not want him to play the flute or drum or any musical instrument like a woman." "Lao Wu [Old Five, a pet name for DaKe], you take the flute back for Uncle [my father] to the principal and explain the situation to him properly." From that moment on, I never played any sort of flute at home till decades later, his daughter, Chin'er, brought one back from her school fete. (She never knew her father could play the Chinese bamboo flute so beautifully even after so many decades later).

Kung Fu Lessons

The principal of the girls' school, Cheng Hsiensen, had started martial arts classes in his school, and he had asked the wusu master from the local army corps to come and be the instructor. The boys had to participate. The classes were held on the other side of the pond at of one of the students' homes. Every morning at five, they had to be at the grounds, line up, and be ready to start with "push hands" exercises immediately. they started with Bo-Lu fists and push hands and practiced for an hour until six; then rushed back to school in time for the mandatory morning exercises. At seven, they returned home for breakfast and at eight returned to school for classes to begin. It was very rigorous for little eight- and ten-year-olds. On Mondays, Tuesdays, and Wednesdays, they practiced kung fu in the mornings; and on Thursdays, Fridays, and Saturdays, they practiced after school, at four in the afternoons. they preferred the afternoon sessions because there were no classes afterward so they could continue to "play" as long as they wanted. I was most interested in BoLu-fist and push-hands techniques because BoLu taught them to protect themselves and attack with great speed. It was during one of these sessions that I met my lifelong friend Wong MungChow who was several years older than me and had been assigned to be his coach/opponent. Martial arts taught the boys to be very fast and agile: the faster, the stronger and better one became. Though he was much younger than MungChow, he was much faster, and his agility allowed him to evade many of MungCHow's strikes, but I landed many blows on him, and his arms were often black-and-blue due to his speedy strikes. The teacher used to apply a special salve to make the bruises disappear overnight. Once, I was practicing push hands against Teacher Chen and lost control of himself. In one backhand motion, he slapped him and knocked him onto the floor, he ran over to him and apologized.

"Never mind, never mind," Teacher Chen said.

The wusu master came over to me and said, "Very good, very good, but there was one error. In opening your arms, you exposed your *tantien* [solar plexus] to attack." He never mentioned about my knocking down Teacher Cheng, instead, I was required to practice how to protect my tantien until sundown. This taught me a lesson: never strike a teacher down! Secretly, I was delighted at my punishment, for I loved to do martial arts.

Cheng Hsien-sen's eldest daughter, ShaFe, was extremely good at the "soft" variety of kung fu, and the boys all admired her and wanted to challenge her—but never dared. She was particularly good at running across the "wave bridge." This was a small suspension wooden bridge built specially for kung fu practice. It was constructed to be deliberately unstable because as soon as one stepped on it and took a few steps, it took on a wave motion. The new boys spent a lot of time being thrown off and having to pick themselves up much of the time. ShaFe, on the other hand, could run across the bridge with no difficulty at all, we could hardly even walk across it. There was one other student who could not only run across it but also jump on to it in one leap. His name was Lung ChungLiang, the assistant to the gym teacher. But for some unknown reason, he was very fond of me and tried to give me private instructions, which I did not really want.

Started English with Koo Hsien-sen

During those years in the late 1920s, China was beginning to open to the world after decades of being closed; relations with England was especially good. The latter could see the potential market in China for imported goods, especially opium!

BaBa told me that it was necessary for him to learn English. Cheng Hsien-sen was a very modern and progressive man. As he knew some English, so his father hired him to come to the house to give his son private English lessons. When Cheng hsien-sen came, I was told to address him as Cheng lao-scee (old teacher), and show him to his room. We started with the alphabets, which, I learned, had twenty-six letters. This was completely new to me, as there were none such in Chinese. He found this most amusing, for even at that young age, I could not see how an entire language could be based on only twenty-six letters. I already knew about three hundred Chinese characters! When we came to the letter *w*, I could not control myself anymore and burst into laughter.

"What is the matter? Why do you laugh?" Cheng lao-scee asked.

"It sounds like *tsan dou*," I replied laughingly.

"How can that be? It does not even sound like *w*."

"No, no not the *tsan* in Chinese but the *tsan-dou.* in the Dawu dialect, it is *nysnew*, which does sound like *w*. In true Tibetan, tsan-dou was called cha-tse-ma [*cha* means *Han*, and *tse-ma* means *beans*] because these beans came from China," I announced. "But I still don't know why it was called *nysnew*," I continued to babble.

"Keep quiet and continue your lesson," reprimanded Cheng laoScee.

A few days later, BaBa met an Englishman by the name of Wellington Cunningham, who had also taken on a Chinese name of Koo FuAn. He was the minister of the local Protestant church. BaBa was very interested in Mr. Koo because he not only knew Chinese but also spoke the proper Khangding dialect and perfect Tibetan. So, I was taken to meet him,

"This is my son, ChiPei, and he is seven years old," BABa said to Mr. Koo when they arrived at his home. "Son, this is Mr. Koo, Koo laoScee."

"No, no, please do not call me laoScee. Call me Hsien-sen instead. I do not like the word *laoscee*. It sounds too much like *rat*, and I hate and am afraid of them. I don't even like to say words that sound like *lao-suu* [*rat* in Chinese]."

I was to begin lessons the very next week for five days a week after school. I was very excited. I already knew the alphabets, so we began by putting them together to form simple words like *cat, dog, rain, book, rice, chalk, chair, table, earth, pond,* and all the words pertaining to our everyday life. I was able to pick them up quickly, and after several weeks, Koo *hsien-sen* and I could have some short simple conversations using those simply everyday words. He was a good teacher; even though he was strict, he was also funny and liked to play simple word tricks. Once, he asked me, "How many fingers do you have in one hand?"

I almost blurted out "Five" but quickly realized that my thumb was not really called a finger, so I replied tartly, "Five."

"All right, do you have a knife?" he asked, eyes twinkling.

"No," I replied, feeling alarmed.

Then one of the other students pulled out a penknife from his pocket, saying, "I have this small one. Will this do?"

Then Koo hsien-sen proceeded to "cut" off my thumb, I pretended to be horrified and shouted, "I have not said anything wrong. Why are you cutting off my thumb?" Then I realized I had said "five" instead of "four."

He laughed and said, "You said you have five fingers, so you have an extra one, so why not cut it off, eh?" I was embarrassed. "Right, if you make a mistake, you must suffer the consequences."

"I will be more careful next time and try not to be so quick and make such silly mistakes again," I boy swore.

Mr. Koo was a Christian and the pastor of the little church. Every Sunday he held services and persuaded the people to come and hear his sermon. He wanted his pupils to go to church also, though most of them were Buddhists. I wanted to go to church because there was a tennis court there and I wanted to learn how to play tennis. So dutifully, I went to church every Sunday, and after the services, most of which I did not understand and often nodded off during the long speeches, though he tried his best to stay awake.

After church and all the snacks were put away, then I was then allowed to go to the tennis court and observe anyone who was playing. It looked like a wonderful game, and I hoped someone would offer to teach me one day. He soon learned the rules of the game and offered to be the "ball boy" to pick up the balls for the players. After several weeks, Mr. Koo finally offered to teach him. It was a very difficult game, and the racket was heavy and large for me, but I persevered and tried very hard and kept my eye on the ball all the time. After many days and numerous attempts, I was finally able to hit a ball over the net.

"Ah! Now you can start to learn to play tennis," said Mr. Koo.

I could not say how happy I was. Over many months, MR. Koo was able to teach me how to receive and return balls, how to serve, how to hit backhand, etc. It was a long and rewarding process, which served me well many years later, when they lived in Calcutta (now Kolkata), India.

One evening he invited his pupils to his quarters to have English tea and cakes. This was the first time I had tasted sweet milky tea, as normally for us, tea was drunk with salt and yak butter. I secretly admitted that I preferred this sweet tea.to the Tibetan salty tea.

Koo also taught him how to play many board games, such as poker, checkers, and chess, which he told said had originated in India hundreds of years ago, and also the ancient Chinese game of Go. All these games I learned to play quite well. Later on in life, he taught them to his son and daughter and even a few of his grandchildren.

"Rotten Stick" Liu NanGau Daifu Cures Typhoid

Mr. Koo was very kind to me, and his affection was returned. His wife, Koo tai-tai (Mrs.), often cleaned and dressed my knees when he fell and scraped them during a tennis game, or brought me delicious English cakes and biscuits (cookie). One day Mrs. Koo came and told me that Mr. Koo was not able to give him a tennis lesson that day because he was ill.

"What kind of illness does he have?" I asked. "Cold?"

"No, typhoid," Mrs. Koo replied.

"What is typhoid?" but she did not know how to answer that question. I ran to the house of Fu laoscee, the upper-grade teacher and the postmaster general of the town, to ask him what was typhoid.

"You should ask your own father, as he is a well-trained herbal doctor himself. Tell him to go and see Mr. Koo. I am sure he will be able to help him."

I replied, "When I had typhoid myself last year, Baba did not treat me but hired an opium-smoking, shoddily-clad, dirty old man called Liu NanGan to treat me. But he did cure me. Why did not my own father treat me?"

"No, our *Daifu* do not treat their own family members, for fear of making a mistake."

Liu NanGan, who was commonly known as Rotten Stick, had a fur jacket so old that most of the fur was worn away. He had never been known to change his garment whatever the weather. I told Mr. Koo about Liu NanGan, and he agreed to let him come and try. But when he brought Liu daifu (medicine man), Mr. Koo changed his mind. He did not want Liu to touch him because of his very dirty appearance. I assured Mr. Koo that he was an extremely good Chinese herbal doctor. Finally, Mr. Koo decided to give him a chance. Reluctantly, he let Liu daifu hold his wrist and feel his pulse for a long time. Then he told Koo *laoscee* to stick out his tongue, which he did gingerly, and Liu looked at it closely; then he diagnosed his illness. He made up a prescription of various kinds of herbs, which he boiled down to fill three cups to be taken in three batches. He offered the first cup to Mr. Koo who took one look at it and turned his face away. This made me very angry, though I was only nine at the time, I was not afraid to speak my mind. He grabbed the bowl of medicine and drank some himself, and commanded, "Mr. Koo, it was you who taught us the Chinese proverb 'The best medicine is bitter to taste but best for the illness,' so drink." At this, Mr. Koo looked at his young stern pupil, then took the bowl, and grimacing, downed it in one gulp. He exclaimed,

"This is the worst soup I have ever eaten in my life," and promptly fell asleep. I said to Mrs. Koo, "I shall return later to help you with laoscee's second dose." She saw me to the door with tears glistening in her eyes. I returned home and told BaBa about the whole thing.

He asked, "Did Liu daifu say anything else?"

I replied," He said that everything would be ready and that only one round of medication was necessary."

His father laughed and said, "So Rotten Stick Liu has such confidence?"

BaBa then said, "I own a six-volume set of books all about typhoid written by Liu ChangKue, the other name for Liu NanGan, Daifu Rotten Stick. "Read it!"

ChiPei took them to his room, but I never read it. What would a nine-year-old boy do with a six-volume set of books dealing with typhoid? When I grew up and matured, Ie often regretted that I did not, and now those volumes are lost forever.

Next day, I went to see Mr. Koo. He was already awake and lying on the chaise lounge. His hair and beard were all tousled, but he was very bright-eyed and spirited and welcomed him with a broad smile.

"Come here, lad," he called.

"Good morning, hsien-sen. How are you? Do you still have a fever?" I asked.

"After I drank that first awful draft of medicine, I started to sweat profusely. But very shortly afterward, my fever broke and started to come down. After the next two doses, I felt as if I were in a bath. Mrs. Koo had to dry me and change my pajamas and bedding several times. Now I feel as if I am the most comfortable person in the world. I thank you for curing my illness."

"No, no, it was not me. It was 'Rotten Stick' Liu *Daifu* who cured you."

Laughingly he said, "Right, it was Liu NanGan who wrote the prescription. But had you not insisted that I see him in the first place, where could I have found such a man? If you had not forced me to drink that awful first dose, I most probably would have died." He continued ponderously, "I must say it is Chinese medicine that cured me. We English are very self-important and consider ourselves better than anyone in the world because we are the largest empire in the world. We have a saying, 'The sun never sets over Great Britain.' In fact, there are many things we do not know or understand. For instance, today I have been cured of typhoid where in England there is no known cure. The only way we know is to wait for the fever to burn itself out, taking anything between three to four weeks. Often the patient just could not tolerate the length of time and expired. In Germany a new medicine is also used, but it is not so effective so far, and many people dare not risk the treatment. Today, if you had not brought your expert, Liu NanGan, and forced me to try him and his Chinese medicine, I would never have had this exceptional experience. It is, indeed, you who introduced Chinese medicine to an arrogant Englishman!" Then he laid back, exhausted.

I was speechless at his praise because he was only doing what he knew. To him, it was nothing special. In fact, they called their so-called expert 'Rotten Stick.' When Mr. Koo recovered, he returned to his teaching duties. One day, after school, he asked me to go home with him, he ran home to get Mma's permission.

When he arrived home and asked Mma, she said, "No, your Baba will be going to Tsan Dwe [in the Tsan Haw District, locally known as NayRun]. Go talk to Baba."

I pleaded, "But I will return very soon. I will not stay long,"

"Oh, all right, quickly go and quickly return," she agreed.

I ran to Mr. Koo's house. He was waiting with a very large sheet of paper printed with English.

"This is Shanghai's 'Western newspaper,'" he said. I had never seen a newspaper before, and this was the only English newspaper in those times. MR. Koo said that he had written an article about his recent typhoid illness and how a Chinese doctor using only Chinese herbal medicine had cured him. He showed me the article in the paper.

"Please tell your father that I admire Chinese medicine and your doctors."

When I returned home, and told BaBa, he only exclaimed, "Do we need him, a foreigner, to praise our medical prowess? Our medical knowledge dates back at least three thousand years to the Warring States of the Three Kingdoms, to Bien Cho and Hwa Tho." Baba continued, slightly annoyed, "It is a pity we ourselves do not appreciate our own knowledge, and not only do we not study the ancient texts and writings, but we also cannot even save what we have. We can only see others improve and grow with our knowledge. At least the foreigners appreciate what we have. What can I say?" He shook his head and sighed a sigh of deep disappointment. I hardly understood what he was talking about and only stood there staring at the floor, dumbfounded.

(NB. BienCho was a daifu (Chinese doctor) who lived during the Three Warring States, about three thousand years ago. One day, as BienCho was walking along a street in his village, he saw a man with a large growth on his forehead. He stopped and looked at the man intensely. The man complained, "Aya, I have a very bad headache. It is as if something is hammering inside my head. I cannot sleep, I cannot think, I do not even enjoy my food. What can I do to stop my head from hurting so? Ayo, ayo," he groaned.

BienCho said, "There is a little bird inside your head doing just that, hammering."

The man left in disgust, but he returned to BienCho a few days later because his pain was so intolerable and no one wanted to touch him.

"You do what you can do to stop this awful pain," he cried to BienCho.

"I will cut open your head," he said.

"Aya, how can you do this? I will surely die," the sick man's family and he cried in alarm.

"I guarantee that there is a bird in your head, and if you want me to stop your pain, then I must open your head and let you see for yourself. It is your decision. Do you want the pain to go away?"

Being in such agony, the man agreed to the operation. Indeed, when the scalp of his head was opened, the pressure caused by a large growth— the 'bird'—flew out. The growth was drained, and pressure released. His scalp was sewn back up again, and the pain was gone. The man was cured of his headache. This was one of the first surgeries performed on any person.

Hwa Tho was another daifu who had lived during the times of the Three Kingdoms Period. He found that Kuang Kung, one of the three main generals, had an arrow in his left biceps, which was already infected. WhaTho realized that if something was not done, this infection would spread throughout the body and the much-feared general would lose his life. It would be a terrible loss to his commander. HwaTho offered to operate on Kuang Kung. Rather than accepting any form of support for his arm, the general simply placed his left hand on his hip and told HwaTho to get on with the surgery. He cut the flesh right down to the bone, which had already turned blackish blue due to the infection, and the smell of the rotting flesh was unbearable. Then HwaTho took his knife and scraped and cut away all the rotten flesh and sewed his arm back again. Without missing a step, Kuang Kung was able to move his arm and returned to battle. HwaTho was amazed at the tremendous bravery and pain tolerance of this amazing general because most people would have fainted.)

Palanquins and Palanquin Rhyming

Early one evening, Mr. Koo had invited Ma TseChao hsien-sen, the principal, and three of his students—Chen SungLing, Fun YouTse, and ChiPei—for tea. He had wanted to show them a special book on palanquins and palanquin rhyming. I was very intrigued, though his fellow students had thought it was a waste of time. Years later, when he had been posted to Burma (now Myanmar) and India, he tried to find this book, but without success. Decades later, in 1976, when his eldest daughter, Pu-Chin, was in London, he had asked her to look for it, and still could not find it. He has since traveled halfway around the world but never found it.

Before cars came to China, in the north, the most advanced form of transportation was by horse and carriage, but in the south where things were even more backward, people rode either horses or donkeys or walked everywhere. If one were slightly rich and were a "better" class of people, one used the palanquins as the method for going long distances. There were two kinds of palanquins: open and closed ones. In the mountainous areas, such as Sichuan and Xikhan, the open varieties were more commonly used. This was simple and more manageable: two long bamboo poles were pushed and strapped to the underside of a simple armchair on which the rider sat, and two people lifted the client up and carried him to his destination. This was called the *wha gan* (open palanquin). Some of the richer clients who could pay more, instead of an armchair, had a large bamboo basket. Not unlike a babies' cradle, it was slung from the poles, and the person was able to "lounge" comfortably in it with cushions and quilts to "soften" the ride. Depending on the size of the client and the speed he wanted to be conveyed, he was carried by four or six men. The second mode of transportation was the "closed" conveyances; these were usually larger and had a boxlike "carriage." Four poles were lashed to the sides of the box. These palanquins were usually used for carrying brides to her wedding or a family moving to another district, or larger more opulent clients. However, no matter the occasion, only the man or two men in the front could see ahead. To let the men behind know what was coming up, he would announce the condition of the road, the traffic, the road surface, the pedestrians—anything that might make a monotonous journey more interesting and fun.

All this was conveyed in rhyme, or "rap," as we would say today. For instance, "Boa-tien-se" or "Hint of little event," the carriers in front would shout, meaning that the ground was uneven and slippery.

The carriers in the back would then shout back in reply, "Sure-footed."

Or if there was a stream ahead, the leader would shout, "Water-rippling," to be replied with "clear and bright"; or if there was a cow pat on the path, "Oh, a flower on the ground."

"Careful where you step" came the response.

The sight of a large animal, such as a cow or horse, "Strong object on your left/right," "So then leave him alone."

If a pretty girl was on the road, "Delicate flower on the left/right," "Let's take her home."

Quite often, friendship struck up between the carried and carriers. The latter would make jokes about their passengers during the journey. These humorous jabs are often beautiful little rhymes, which the local folks considered as nothing special, but Mr. Koo found them fascinating and had translated many of these rhymes into English. These were published in London, but which I have never been able to find.

Mr. Koo, at the age of seventy-one, having lived over half a century in China, finally left. I shall always remember his final words: "China is truly an ancient and literary nation that even the lowly palanquin bearers could speak in rhyme spontaneously."

Mr. Koo had a fellow minister called Mr. Yeh, who was a member of the English Astronomical Society, a totally absentminded scientist. He used to assist Mr. Koo in his ministerial affairs. This Mr. Yeh never combed his hair and beard. His shirt was torn, and his trousers had holes.

Whether he walked in front or behind you, you always knew it was Mr. Yeh. He held a stick in his right hand, which he used to ward off stray dogs. In his left hand, he had a pair of large binoculars, which he put up to his eyes to peer into the sky, whatever the time of day or night. He loved Dawu because he said that it was the blackest sky he had ever been under. My friends and I could never understand what was the meaning of this "blackest sky" until I grew up and lived in a large city with many lights at night and then the sky was no longer inky black. The adults used to call him foreign beggar, while we children called him goat man because the words *goat* and *foreign* in Chinese sounded alike—*yang-ren*, thus "goat man." Indeed, some of the younger children thought that he was a reincarnation of a goat.

In those remote places, such legends were common, and people were often subdued by such uncommon happenings, and children who didn't want to go to bed at night, were told that "the monster with red hair and green eyes will catch you." My daughter Pu-Chin was threatened with such a monster until she met such a man from Ireland. She thought he was the handsomest man she had ever seen.

One particularly brave youngster crept up behind Mr. Yeh to stroke this goat man's rear, but he jumped back, greatly alarmed. "Aya, this is a *jui-lee-tse*," meaning a short-tailed or no-tail goat. All the children ran up behind Mr. Yeh and tried to touch him. Mr. Yeh was furious and ran back to Mr. Koo, shouting, "These people are too savage. I cannot continue to live here." In a few days, he left, and they never saw him again. Poor fellow.

Mr. Koo asked if any of the older children had participated in teasing Minister Yeh. Of course, everyone denied it and claimed that they would form a gang and go and beat up those "wild and ill-mannered boys." Mr. Koo warned me that I should not take sides because he knew that I was not like those children, who, when I was either going to or coming from school, would push me and strike me from behind because my father was richer and more privileged than theirs and my hair was curly. However, I knew that if they actually faced me, none of them could beat me because of my kung fu skills. But I was one against many, so I could only "grin and bear" their bullying.

During physical exercises one morning, Mr. Koo told me that one of those boys who was playing soccer in the field had kicked a ball into the yard of a neighbor. This neighbor refused to return the ball, and his son had taken a sharp object and punctured the ball.

"That is Hwa ChungJuin's house."

"Yes," said Mr. Koo, "that is right."

I realized that there was a slight antagonism between Mr. Koo and his best friend. I felt very bad, so I went to ask ChungJuin whether this was true.

"This is not the first time," complained ChungJuin. "Time and time again, balls were kicked into our house. They even knocked over and broke my mother's flower pots. I had complained of this to Mr. Koo several times, but he never took any notice of me. This is not my fault. It is the fault of the players."

I listened then said, "I will ask Mr. Koo to tell them to play field hockey and volleyball instead of soccer."

Fortunately, Mr. Koo agreed; and for a time, a truce was reached.

The Americans: Andersons and Electric Bulbs

One afternoon Chiang KoSen, a schoolmate seven older than me, asked,

"Do you want to meet a few Americans children —Bobby, Susie, and Jenny—whose father was Dr. Anderson.

"Bobby is eight years old. Susie and Jenny are seven and five," said KoSen.

"Oh, I know Dr. Anderson," I said.

"How do you know him?"

"I met him at Mr. Koo's when we were playing tennis."

"Oh," exclaimed KoSen incredulously.

"No, no, I could not play tennis against them. I was only the scorekeeper and ball boy," I said, smiling.

"Then I will take you to meet the Anderson children. They have been here for so many years and have not made many friends. I am sure you will like them, and they will like you, and we can become friends." The Anderson house was the only one that had electricity because they had a generator. We considered this fantastic. I had never seen an electric lightbulb and never imagined how it worked. Their front gate was in the shape of a pair of wings, and the surrounding wall was only half the normal height. The house itself was in the middle of a garden, which was filled with the most beautiful flowers with names I did not know. The ground was covered with long soft grass just like the hair on the wolf skins we used on our floors. On the edge of the garden was a creek with clear fast-flowing water. The creek flowed through a small building, which housed the generator, and then out again. KoSen brought the three children toward me and introduced them in order of age: Bobby, Susie, and Jenny. Bobby was slightly shorter than me.

"I'm eight," he said.

"And I am nine," I said. "So you must call me KeKe [elder brother]."

"No, no," he protested, "we don't call like that. We just say hi."

Then he introduced me to Susie, who had a headful of golden hair and eyes the color of the sky. She was a beautiful girl. The last one was the littlest sister, five-year-old Jenny.

Among them, only Bobby could say a few words in Chinese. He said that they ate dinner at six o'clock, but by five thirty, they must go into their house, wash up and pray before their meal. They played on the swing, which was different, because their swing had a board on the bottom fixed with two ropes, and one could only swing back and forth but to a great height. The local swings consisted only of a large rope hanging from a tree and with a big knot at the bottom. We grasped it with both hands and swung north, south, east, and west. As long as you hung on, you could go in any direction.

I turned and asked Bobby, "Do you grind your own wheat in your millhouse?"

Looking at the small building through which the stream ran, he had no idea what I was talking about. He pointed to what he thought was a millhouse.

"Oh that! That is not a millhouse. That is where the light comes from at night. Do you not have lights in your house at night?" he asked incredulously.

"Yes," I replied proudly, "we have not only candles but also oil lamps."

"Oh, we do not have those. Our light comes out of a machine." I was astonished and did not understand at all. "I will show you someday when you come into our house one night," Bobby said.

"Oh, thank you. I would love to see lights come out of a machine," I said, full of enthusiasm.

At that moment, their mother called them in for dinner. "Thank you for coming to play with my children," said their mother dressed in a strange short dress with lots of flowers on the cloth, just like her garden. "Please come and play again."

Before we left, I looked around in their home and saw some glass-like balls hanging from the ceilings. These glass balls suddenly radiated a red glow, which turned gradually yellow, then very bright, much brighter than any oil lamps or candles he had ever seen. His disbelief showed on his astonished face.

Mrs. Anderson smiled and said, "These are electric bulbs. Today it is late. Come earlier tomorrow, and I will explain to you about these lights."

"Thank you," still filled with wonder. "I will ask Mr. Koo about them."

"All right." She said, "Good night. Do come again."

We all said bye-bye; then KoSen and I returned to our own candlelit houses, which, suddenly, seemed terribly dim.

Later, I asked Mr. Koo "Have you seen that little building near their house? Is that the electricity-producing machine? Why don't you build a small light making house like the Andersons?"

"Did you see the stream in their garden?" asked Mr. Koo. "That stream comes from Tse UrPoh, the waterfall, and flows through their garden. They constructed a machine over that stream and use the fast-running water for power to produce electricity. We do not have any stream or any form of flowing water on our property. Therefore, we cannot produce electricity. It was a scientist called Thomas Edison, in 1847, who first discovered electricity, and later, he made it available worldwide." He sighed. "There are very important events happening in the world today, and alas, I am too old to participate. It all depends on you young ones now."

I did not totally understand what he was talking about and what he had meant by depends on 'you young ones.' I only knew that he loved our village and its people, that he wanted the villagers to share in all the progress that is happening in the world.

Soldiers in Town

One day BABA called his son to his office, which terrified me, because I was never allowed in his office. I tried to cast in my mind as to what I had done to make him angry with me. I trembled as I walked to his father's office door.

"ChiPei, *lai lai*, I have something to tell you." I went in and stood to attention in front him. Then he told me that he had been transferred to the Tsan Hwa District where there was some unrest. "But before I officially take up my new position, we must move to a larger house because your Second Uncle and his family will also be staying with us." Baba had arranged with Chiang BeiBei who owned a very large house for us to rent and occupy the left tower wing of the manor. We were to live in the upper floors while our horses and horse keepers were on the ground floor. My second uncle and his family would have their own apartment in the right tower wing. Baba said, "I will be away on duty very often, so Second Uncle will be able to keep an eye on Mma, and Second Uncle's wife will

49

be able to help the maids take care of you and DaJieh [my elder sister]." I was happy because he was to have another (cousin) sister to tease. Baba was employed directly by the Emperor's office as the protectorate of the southwestern border provinces to keep the bandits and robbers out of the region and the citizens safe from them.

One day, while Baba was on one of his missions, Second Uncle returned from work earlier than normal and immediately asked Mma to pack up and go to the Catholic Church. He and his wife then took me and his two sisters and their maidservants and went to the south gate of the church. There, they appointed them to a room, which was huge and in which many other families had already gathered. Their family was told to assemble in a small corner of the room; then Second Uncle and I went to the bishop's office to ask what had happened. He did not have any answers, only told them to keep very quiet and wait. When it was dark, our family was sent to the abbey. There was a hospital there, and Second uncle and I were put into a separate hospital room. Our stay there was totally inconvenient and uncomfortable. At six in the evening, the door was locked from the outside so that I could not even go to see Mma and Jiehjieh. It was all very confusing to everyone. No one had told them anything or tried to explain as to why they were brought there and what they wanted with them. After several hours, I was at last allowed to go and see Mma and Jiehjieh, but I had to returned to my hospital room at 6:00 p.m. At nine o'clock, all the lights were turned off, and every was left in total darkness. It was even more stressful for second Uncle because he was an opium smoker and accustomed to his daily evening smokes. all the windows and doors had to be sealed so that no one saw his light and smoke. When I was sure that Uncle was "out," he climbed out of the window and went into town to see what was going on. When he returned, Uncle was awake and very angry, for he had been worried and afraid.

"You should have told me before you went out," he admonished.

"I did not want to worry you, and I just wanted to find out what was going on outside and why we were locked here in this church." I added, "the people were all right but there are many soldiers milling about the village, and there were strange people living in their house, but did not know to why.

After that, I often went back to his house and gradually made "friends" with the captain of the soldiers who had commandeered their house. He had a small dog with fur like black satin, and it had a tail that stuck straight up and ended in a tight curl. The captain said that he would give it to me when they left. Uncle then asked whether they had asked about their family.

"Yes, they had." I told him that they were from Dawu.

"Where is Dawu?" the captain had asked.

"It is not far. It takes only several days to get there from here"

"How did you learn to speak such good Chinese?"

"Teacher taught me in school," I lied instinctively.

"Okay," Uncle said, "you did good. Just do not say too much, and do not go there again."

However, I continued to sneak out during the day instead of at night. But was still unable to find out why those soldiers were in their house or what they were doing in this remote town.

One day there was a sign posted at the town gate: "Found one lost white sheep. Come and claim it if it is yours."

I went up to the guard and asked, "Where is the sheep?"

"It is in the Ministry of Finance" came the answer.

"What? Where is that?" pretending ignorance.

"Up ahead, you will come across a large, tall wall. Beside that is the Ministry of Finance," he said sternly.

Then as I headed that way, he suddenly shouted, "Hey, are you not a local boy. How stupid you are if you do not even know that."

I did not answer but kept walking. I knew that it was my sheep they were holding. I went to the Ministry of Finance, and indeed, there was a sheep held with a rope beside the stables. It was my pet sheep with a small red blanket on its back, which the second maid had made for it. I went toward the stables to collect my pet.

"Where do you think you are going, and where are you taking that sheep?" shouted a soldier.

"This is my sheep. The sign said to claim it if it were your sheep. It is mine," I replied firmly.

"And how do you know that? Can you prove it?"

"But of course, I can. My sheep listens to me," I retorted indignantly. "If he does not know you, he will not listen to you."

The soldier laughed. "Wait here," he said and went to the stables and brought with him a bearded old man and said, "This boy says that the sheep belongs to him because it listens to him. Ha-ha-ha."

Peering at me, the bearded man said, "What do you mean 'listens' to you, eh, eh, eh? Eh, listens to you, eh?"

"Let him go, and I will call him by his name, and he will come to me."

"Okay, let the sheep loose. Call your sheep. If it does not listen to you, then it's your own fault, and it is not your sheep!"

I said confidently, "That will not happen." When the soldier loosened the sheep, he called, "Kala, Kala."

The sheep looked around, bleated, and immediately ran over to him, rubbed itself on his legs, and licked him, all the time bleating, "Maa, maa, maa."

The bearded old man scratched his beard, patted my head, smiled, and said, "It is indeed your sheep, but be quick. Take it home before anyone else put a claim on it. Then it will be difficult to get him back."

I ran away followed by his sheep, and as he passed the guard and the old man, he heard them laugh out loudly. I took my sheep to my house. The small horse boy was surprised to see his young master with KalaKala. He told me that when he was taken away, the sheep had run away and did not return home. He must have gone to look for you, and because the streets were so confusing during those days with all the soldiers and other out-of-towners, it must have become totally confused and lost.

"I thought someone must have caught it, killed and eaten it," said the horse boy, who then hugged me and wept with joy. The whole family, except for him, did not like Kala Kala because it followed me everywhere, even into my bedroom. He bleated a lot and tended to butt people if he was annoyed. Except for me, he was a nuisance to everyone else. The only other person who loved him as much as was his horse boy; he even shared his straw bed with this pet. When the second maid chased KalaKala downstairs from my bedroom, the small horse boy scolded him for going upstairs to the human's living quarters. In fact, no one in the family cared for our animals as much as the small horse boy and me. Whenever we entered the stables, the horses grunted welcomes and nodded in greeting, and the sheep ran/hopped over to butt affectionately.

One evening I heard uncle and auntie discuss that if something serious were to happen, they would take me to father. At that time and age, I did not understand what was the meaning of "change or no change." What was wrong with being the same all the time? Again, he stole out of the church grounds and into town to his home. When he arrived, the servants shook his hands happily and said, "They are gone, all gone now."

"Who are all gone?"

"That captain and his soldiers."

"Did they move into another house? Can we come home now? and where did they go?" I did not understand.

"They left early this morning, and said that they will never return."

"The captain said that he would leave me his little black dog when they leave, and I did not even ask for it, so where is it?"

"We do not know anything about that. He left last night with his dog."

I was most disappointed. How can one believe an adult's words? I could not understand anything. I had so many unanswered questions in mind, not least as to why our house had been taken over by those soldiers and we were moved into the Catholic Church. In fact, what were the soldiers doing here in such a remote part of China?

During those years, there was conflict between the Nationalist Party under Dr. Sun Yat-sen who had overthrown the Manchu dynasty but was now threatened by a new uprising of the Communists under Mao Tse Tung, who was walking across the country from the south, where he came from, toward the capital, Beijing in the north. Thousands of supporters joined him on this Long March along the way, and it was rumored that he may march through Sichuan and Sikhang; thus, soldiers were posted around these rather remote regions as a precaution against possible uprisings.

Chapter 3

Return To Dawu

Second Uncle took Auntie, the cousin sister, my mother, sister and me back to their own house in town rather than back to the Chiangs' manor. They lived on the street near the south gate. Baba returned, and brought with him many soldiers, so it was not convenient for everyone to live in their home. He set up camp outside the town with his soldiers. So, the rest of the family went to live with Second Uncle. There were three main bedrooms. My mother, sister and I shared the largest bedroom facing the street; Uncle and Auntie stayed in the smaller room in the back. My older cousin sister lived in a tiny room beside theirs, and I realized, even then, that she was a very unhappy girl ever since her mother died several years ago. She never got over it.

A few days later, Mma told me that BaBa was returning on the morrow and that we would be moving again, this time to a larger house with a bigger compound. Second uncle and his family could live in a separate building, but within the same compound. BaBa had also rented the building across the street where his soldiers could live; their sheep and horses were left, for the time being, in the Chiangs' compound.

Then Mama told me that during the past several weeks of upheaval and political unrest, their house had been commandeered by the army for their use. Fortunately, the Catholic Church was able to give us shelter, for which we were very thankful. As an act of gratefulness, Uncle suggested that I give me sheep to the bishop. I was most unwilling.

"If you are unwilling," said his mother, "then Baba will slaughter the sheep for his soldiers for food. You know that they are perfect marksmen, as if their hands were 'guided by heaven.' With one shot, Kala will be gone! Did you know that Baba trained them to shoot only the enemies' left hands rather than kill one single man? Your father did not like to kill anyone. He preferred to frighten away their enemies rather than kill them."

When I heard this, I understood what his mother was trying to tell him. He immediately decided to give his sheep to the bishop. Later, he heard that and sheep and some other farm animals s in the Catholic compound were kept for reproduction, not for meat. Next day, they took KalaKala to the bishop's house. The bishop saw us walking up and saw that the sheep was quietly following behind. Amazed, he said,

"What are you doing here. What a clever sheep you have – following like a dog."

"This is a gift for you, Father," I said, "for giving us shelter and safety when we were in trouble. But will you kill it and eat it?" he asked with some trepidation.

The priest smiled and said, "No, no, we will not kill it or eat it. Our sheep are free to run about and play in our compound." He assured me.

I was relieved and jumped with joy, at which the bishop added, "You have a kind heart, dear boy, and God will protect and bless you."

"I am a student of Mr. Koo," thinking that the bishop, like Mr. Koo, was a Christian and, therefore, the same. I had no idea that there were so many kinds of Christians.

"I am not a Protestant. I am a Catholic," said the bishop, "but it does not matter. God and Jesus are all the one God. Take the sheep to our compound and let him join his new friends."

I turned to my sheep and said, "KalaKala, don't run away again." When I turned to leave, he ran after me, "Maa, maa," and tried to follow me. I ran back and hugged it. The bishop saw this and was touched and said, "There is really no need to give us anything."

"This is our gratitude for letting us stay in your church during the recent political crisis, and also this is one way I can save my sheep from being eaten! His name is KalaKala. It will come when you call him by his name."

The bishop smiled and invited us into his house and bid us to sit down on his soft seats like sitting on small pillows, which were different from the hard wooden stools and benches we usually used. He poured

Uncle a glass of a dark red drink and a small glass for me. It was slightly sweet and good, so I drank it all in one gulp, and before I knew it, he was fast asleep under the table where they found me.

One Kitchen, Two Families

Mma had told me to stay with Uncle because she was afraid that something would happen to Big Sister. "Do not to fear because as long as she has me, I would protect her." Then Mma asked, "Do you know who gave birth to Big Sister?"

"Xiao yi-nyan,"

"No, not Little Auntie," his mother said.

"Oh, of course not, da yi-nyan did," I replied firmly, suddenly understanding.

Then Mma said, "At night, do not let anyone into her room."

"I have Baba's sword, the one that was used to fight someone. The blood is still on it, dried and caked on. Such a sword will ward off evil. I will put it under my pillow." "Oh no, there is no need for that," cried Mma in alarm. "Put the sword away. It is too dangerous, and you may make a mistake and harm someone."

"Yes," said Uncle who came into the room and saw me with the sword. "That sword did indeed kill someone, but you may keep it to ward off evil. It is not a killer sword anymore." Big Sister beckoned to me, I rushed to her side.

"What is the matter?"

She said quietly, "A thousand million times, do not argue with your little auntie. You must always do as she asks."

"Someone said that you will run away, so I must lock you in your room. Are you to be treated like a thief? I will not do that," I said stubbornly, "Also, I have brought my 'ward-off evil sword,' and I will put it under my pillow. It will ward off any evil."

Big Sister smiled and said, "Scee-Dee [Fourth Younger Brother), I know your intentions are good, but swords cannot always be hidden, and if Third Uncle finds it [that is what my cousin sister called my father], he will spank you."

"Then what shall I do?" I asked.

"You can tell Little Auntie to lock her own door at night."

"Have you ever argued with her?"

"No."

"Then you must have sworn at her and cursed her."

"No, even that no."

"Then why does she not like you?"

"It is entirely my fault." Big Sister became teary eyed and said, "The year before my mother died, my elder brother and I were in ChengDu. Elder Brother was working in the post office, and my father was afraid that I would be lonely, so he brought me to Lucheng [Khangdin]. However, before I arrived in ChengDu, my father had taken the Cheng family's servant girl to be his concubine, and when Ma died, she became his second wife—Little Auntie. My father told me to call Little Auntie 'Mama,' which I refused. So, it is entirely my fault."

"Oh, I understand now."

Big Sister shook her finger at me and smiled. "Be a good boy."

I lowered my head, hummed and haa-ed, and reluctantly said, "Okay, I will be good."

"Scene-Dee, this is my life. Your big sister's life is bitter. Let it be." She put her hands to her face, and her shoulders shook as she softly sobbed into her hands. I put my arms around her and comforted her. I locked DaJieh's door as he was told. His mother shook her head with much sadness.

One day, at dinner, Bei-sao, our servant girl, whispered something in Mma's ear, who exclaimed loudly, "This cannot be." Shaking her head, she continued, "Little Auntie said that the food is all cold and inedible."

BaBa said, "Go ask Second Lord what would Second Wife like to eat, and then go and tell the kitchen to make it." But before the maidservant left, Uncle arrived, panting and exclaiming, "Chu Nan, I am going to call the owner of the palanquin to come and take her back to her mother's house. She seems to be so unhappy here. I am sorry for this."

Baba quickly said, "Da-Ke [Elder Brother], let it be. This is a small matter." He continued, "Perhaps she is not well. Maybe we should get a doctor to come and have a look at her."

After things calmed down a bit, Yi-Nyan (small Aunty) sent for her own servant, Sen-ma, to the kitchen to prepare the dishes that she liked for her only. Sen-ma was full faced, big hands and feet, and excessively "humble and servile." Whenever she saw anyone, she bent over double in false obeisance; she particularly liked to flatter me by calling him the Fourth Prince, which I disliked. BaBa's personal servant Yan Tsancheng, like a British batman, often warned His master and the rest of the soldiers of Small-ma's ways. "Never mind, let her be. They will not be here long," remarked said kindly.

All the soldiers whom Baba had brought back were returned to Tsan Dow except for Yan Tsancheng. Baba decided that our families and Uncle's family should live in separate houses. I was worried for my older cousin sister, so I told Mma about my concerns, Mma told Baba. After some consideration, he spoke to Uncle,

"My wife's health is not too good and is often weak and sickly. I wonder if you could let your daughter come and live with us to help take care of her. I am being transferred to LuDing District, and I cannot take my family with me. If your daughter were to be with my wife and the younger children, I shall feel very relieved and comforted to know that she is around." My uncle immediately agreed, and so my DaJieh moved in with us, and we were all very happy.

Baba left for his new post, leaving the cook, old Cheng; the maidservants; and a guard to look after the family. He also left a little seven-year-old orphan girl Baba had brought back from one of his sojourns. This little girl was wandering around the countryside and was totally lost, so Baba brought her back to be a servant for Hsueh Taitai. She had a plump little face, large round eyes, thick lips, and a mass of tousled uncontrollable hair filled with lice. She was always smiling and wanted to please. Alas, she also wet her bed every night so that it was always damp, no one liked to go into her little room because of the smell of urine, but Mma grew very fond of her, and the family realized that she genuinely had no one in the world, which was why she was so fearful all the time. Gradually, everyone in the household also grew to like her. Mma tried to teach her Chinese and called her CheungLo (Spring Cheer), and later a slightly older child was hired to help her with her chores. This child did not want to share her room and sleep with her because of the bedwetting problem, but there was no alternative. However, the longer CheungLo was with the family, the less fearful she was, the more settled and happier she became, finally her bedwetting stopped. The new girl was very helpful all around, so we called her Ren Gu-nyan (Everyone's girl). Later, Yi Bei-nyan gave birth to a baby boy and wanted DaJieh to go and help. Mma, however, sent Ren Gu-nyan instead. When we were leaving Khanding, Ren Gu-nyan came to bid us a teary farewell. We never saw her again.

Yu-Ling Kung—Er Dao Chiao

About forty li (thirteen miles) south of Khangding was the Yu-Ling Kung where there were some natural hot springs. Unfortunately, this was too far from town, so few people went there. But just two miles out of the north gate of KhangDing, there was a bridge called Er-Dao Bridge (Second Path Bridge) where there was another hot spring. The townspeople had built a very nice "roof" over a part of the hot spring, and this was where most people came to bathe. My and I considered the sheltered section under the bridge as "our" special place and went there at least once a week. Some Saturdays, if we did not have many classes, we spent all day there. The water was extremely hot, and in one particular place, we used to boil a chicken in half an hour, and we often boiled eggs there for snacks. Skirting a gentle slope on the way to the bridge lived several local and Chinese families, and passing a large rock outcrop, there stood a house whose windowpanes were pasted pieces of paper with large Chinese characters:

Moon shines brightly on window glass

Clear water flow over the rock.

I recognized the couplet at once, a Tang dynasty poem by Wong Wei. I went up to the house and knocked on the door. There was an old man in a long navy-blue cotton robe. He had a long gray beard, which blended with his long gray hair. Even his eyebrows and lashes were gray, and though he seemed very old, his eyes were as bright and piercing as a brightly lit star.

I said to him boldly, "Old Grandpa, you made an error in your writing."

"What, what?" he said agitatedly. "What error did I write? What are you talking about? What?"

"That couplet of the Tang poems should read, 'Moon shines bright on pine trees,' not *windows*. How can it be?"

The old man burst out laughing and said, "You are right, but I am also right."

I was confused. How can we both be right? "Did I remember the couplet incorrectly?" I thought.

Then the old gray beard asked, "You see the mountain there? What direction is it?"

"East," I replied, puzzled.

"Where does the moon rise from?"

"East," still confused.

"What direction does my window face?"

"East."

"So, when the moon rises, where does it shine?" He twinkled.

"On the window," I replied sheepishly and immediately bowed my head and apologized for my brashness.

The old grandpa smiled again and said, "I did not use the Tang poem word for word, so there you are right, and I am also right, as I explained." Then looking at me kindly, he said, "Little Brother," having just called me "little boy. I put up this couplet a long time ago, and this is the first time anyone has taken any notice. Are you by any chance related to Hsueh Tsan Hur or Hsueh Kung Yu?"

"Yes, he is my Er-Bei [second uncle]." It turned out that they had been workmates.

"Ah please, when you see your Er-Bei, tell him White-Bearded old Fung, out of the city gates, sends greetings. Hey, those friends of yours must be bored waiting for you."

"It is all right. We are riding [horses] to Er-Dao Chiao, and it is not very far from here."

He was very reluctant to see me go and slowly closed the door as if he still wanted to say something else but could not speak out.

Twenty years later, in Ding Tan, Anhwei, I met a certain Mr. Fung who had come to succeed me at his post. Mr. Fung took one look at me and called me brother, took me in his arms and wept. Fung was also called Wong YienHung, who had been his classmate in KhangDing. This younger Mr. Fung was the old White-Bearded Fung's son who had been given to the Wong family to bring up because he himself had been alone and too poor to bring up his own son. So that was why Old Grandpa Fung was reluctant to let me go. He had reminded him of his own son— same age, same school—and he was unable to be with him or tell me of his tragidy.

Facing Fung's uncle's house was the GoDa Mountains, below which was an enormous grassy meadow, and in front of this meadow was a crystal-clear river where one could see right down into the riverbed. On either side of the riverbank were tripod structures of thick bamboo deeply and securely anchored into the ground. A very strong rope made of split bamboos was attached to the tripods on either side of the bank. A very large bamboo culm was threaded through the rope, and from the middle of the bamboo tube was a thick rope made of jute, as thick as a man's wrist; at the bottom of this rope hung a bamboo platform just large enough for a man to sit cross-legged. To cross this river, the person put the bamboo culm under his arm and sat on the little bamboo platform and pulled himself across on the split bamboo rope. The local people called this form of crossing *liu sotse*, or "slippery rope crossing." Long ago, in the Sichuan border areas, all rivers were crossed in this manner. If the mountains were too steep, without a wide verge at the base, then these ropes were hung in a crisscross manner. I loved the meadow on the other side and often wanted to go over to see the herds of cattle, sheep, and the small dwellings scattered up the hillsides. As he watched he saw someone slide down the rope. She looked like their servant girl, Bei-sao.

"Are you Bei-sao?" He shouted.

When she saw me, she shouted back, "What are you doing here, #4 Prince, so early in the morning?" I did not like to be called by the title, so I shouted back, "Do not address me like that again, or I will tell your husband, Bei TsaiLe, that you sneaked out from home!"

"All right, Small Master, I will not call you Fourth Prince again."

"Okay, but you must take me to your place to play. I like your side of the river very much."

"Sure, sure, only if your mother agrees."

Then my friends and I mounted ourr horses, galloped a while, and arrived at a gently sloped area between the mountain and river. I was riding a chestnut belonging to Mr. Tung, and when he shouted "Choo, choo," the horse opened his gait and flew like a cloud. Suddenly, I heard our small stable boy, Mau, right behind me say, "Quick." In a flash, our own Bei-Yuin (White Cloud) zoomed ahead. My chestnut sped up and almost caught up to Bei-Yuin but was still three lengths behind. At last, our small *mafu* (horse boy) turned around and stuck out his tongue at me and grimaced at me, saying, "Do you think you can beat our Old Dragon?"

Our Bei-Yuin, affectionately called Old Dragon, was famous throughout the district for his beauty and his speed. When we used to race her at Dawu, she always came first; but since Baba was the one who also handed out the prizes at the end of the races, Bei-Yuin never received his just award in case Baba was accused of favoritism. He was not allowed to run competitively but only for fun. But everyone in town knew he was the fastest horse.

Bei-Yuin was a mountain horse, so he was not very tall but extremely sure-footed. He had a large head and thick neck and was rather short bodied. His legs were long and ended in round hooves. His tail was thin and fine. Often, I would see and hear MauMau, the small mafu, lift up one of Bei-Yuin's hooves in admiration and tell the other horses, "See how ugly you all are."

One day Bei-Yuin suddenly took ill and lay down in his stall and refused to get up. I went to see him, took his head in my lap, and wept; he snorted a little as if to say, "stop crying." He tried to lift his head once and snorted again, "Good-bye, Small Master," and put his head down and died. MauMau was inconsolable, and our entire household fell into a deep sadness so that the village wondered what tragedy had befallen their family. They had thirty horses, but Old Dragon was everyone's favorite. During those times, most people owned several horses because they were the main form of transportation, just like our cars today.

Er-Dao Bridge and the Kuan-Yin Temple

There were other reasons other than the hot spring water to take us boys to the Er-Dao Chiao: first, to race our horses because the distance of the long meadow along the river was perfect for galloping; second, to have water fights in the spring and cook eggs and chicken in the hottest part of the pool; and, third, to visit Kuan-Yin Temple where we could feast on freshly fried sweet pretzels and other delicacies from the vendors on the grounds of the temple. The caretaker of the temple especially like us and would tell the vendors to fry fresh pretzels on the spot for us.

Around Er-Dao Chiao, there were about one hundred families living in fortified dwelling compounds called *ko-tsung*. The largest ones were like the European castles. They could contain a hundred heads of cattle, scores of horses, and at least three living apartments. Some of these were often used as inns, as there were no hotels in the town then. During the summer months, most travelers were tea merchants from ChengDu, known as

YunChing, going to sell their tea in Khanding. I remember those heavily laden donkeys with large sacks on either side of their torso, trudging along the dirt roads. Their masters—stripped to the waist, dripping with sweat—would hurry them along by prodding their sides or gently stroke their rear ends with a whip. They had come a long way. The best teas were branded with the names of the YuFu and Chiang Kung Hsin, who also had branches in Lhasa, then called RenTsin Dorje. If these companies were still active today, they would be close to two hundred years old now.

There was a difference between Big Meadow and Khangding/ Lucheng. The landscape around Big Meadow was wild and desolate. As soon as People left the gates of Big Meadow, and approached LuCheng, they thought they had arrived at some strange and great city, they marveled at the buildings, shops, and numerous eating places. Ed-Dao Chiao was situated right between the two regions was like a dividing line: the lifestyle and culture in LuCheng was entirely Han Chinese while that of outside the city gates was Kham-Tibetan. In fact, nothing had changed much since the Han dynasty till the time I was growing up there; perhaps, things and relations between the two cultures have improved since then.

The Parrot on Beehive Street

Lucheng/Khangding was situated between two mountain peaks with a very fast and extremely cold river running through. From the YuLing Palace and the wild forest, the fast-rushing river comes through the south and the east gates. The town was divided in half by this river into North and South Lucheng. This river joined another one at the base of GoDa Mountain and was the confluence of many rivers and together flowed into the TaDu Ho at LuDin District. At Lucheng, there were four bridges. The southernmost was below YaMeng Street and was called the General Bridge, which had carved pillars and arched railings. I used to think this was the most beautiful bridge in the world. North of the General Bridge was the YaMeng itself, and south of this was the South Gate Main Street. On this street, there used to be a pancake restaurant whose sesame seed cake was famous throughout the district, though I was not as impressed by the pancakes as I was by the couplet posted on their main door. It was strange and very funny:

With a string of copper coins around my waist,

I am spiritually strong;

With three puffs of smoke,

I am so very cultured.

Later, I learned that the owner of this pancake house was an opium addict and might have had some education. He had felt rather inadequate and envious of others more educated, but when he was under the fog of opium, he felt he was equally cultured and educated than those.

Above General Bridge was the second bridge, and at the base of which was our property, so we could easily see people walking along the bridge. This was a very busy thoroughfare. People coming and going to and from Bei TuKan, Ming Tsen TuScee, and SanScee Streets must go via this bridge; otherwise, they would have to make a very wide detour to get from one bank to the other. The wooden slats on this bridge were well worn, some even rotten and broken. Whenever I had to use this bridge, I used to dismount and lead my horse across very carefully, making sure the hooves did not go through one the many missing slats. Down from the bridge was Beehive Street, which was considered the city center. Here was the Center Bridge, the third bridge; to me, this was the most exciting place of the city: restaurants, offices, groceries, general goods stores, and many, many other types of shops and stores. The street here was always crowded with vendors touting all kinds tempting things, anything from sweet pretzels to fried dumplings, from spinning pin-wheels to operatic masks; there were also street performers such as acrobats, martial art combats, magicians etc. Of course, one must be wary of the swift fingered pickpockets. It was wonderful for little boys from the countryside. Alas, there was a sad story connected with this bridge. The owner of the general goods store had a pet parrot who spoke Chinese and Tibetan and could even look after the store for its owner when he was gone for a little while. When it saw a Chinese customer, he would shout, "Aachado, how are you?" in the Khanding dialect; but if he saw a Tibetan enter the store, he would shout, "Kun su do mo ze be," in Tibetan. I supposed he could differentiate the people by their costumes. The Chinese usually wore long unbelted mandarin gowns, and the Tibetans wore their gowns pulled higher to reveal wool boots, and they were usually belted at the waist. The right sleeve was tucked under the belt to expose the right arm, making it easier to hold a horsewhip or a weapon. The proprietor loved his parrot and considered it his living treasure. One day, as I was passing his shop, I saw a large crowd gather in front of it. The proprietor was crying bitterly. I squeezed in and heard that his parrot had been poisoned.

He groaned, "My parrot was too clever. Many times, he had warned me about thieves in the store, and I was able to catch them and take them to the police station. One of these thieves, hated my poor parrot, and when he was let out of jail, he came and poisoned my poor guard with opium seeds." He began to strike his head and wept and wept. The people were appalled and could not believe him, so the proprietor showed the gathered crowd the uneaten seeds left in the parrot's feeding bowl.

I was outraged and at once asked him, "Do you know who is the man who poisoned your bird? I will find him and will avenge your parrot."

"Small Brother, I know to what family you belong, but this is a grown-up's business. You cannot help. But I thank you for your kind heart. Even my parrot thanks you." And he started to bawl again. Some of the people also began to weep but gradually dispersed. I returned home and told Mma what had happened. She shook her head sadly and remarked, "The hearts of the people in this world are too bad, too bad."

From the center of town and continuing on Beehive Road, to the Water-well and north to the FuHo Tea Company, past the Temple Liu Bei (also known as Wong KungChung), and going further down past the district government offices, one arrived at the Kong FuTse (Confucius) Temple. Here spanned the oldest bridge, called the Low Bridge. Much of it was broken and dangerous to use. At the northern end, there was a slope, and the river made a sudden turn to exit through the East Gate. Many people committed suicide from this point, so it was an eerie place. My friends and I almost never crossed this bridge. At the eastern passage was one of the two border checkpoints. The other was at the north gate, and anyone going in or out of town had to have the luggage examined. Later, my father controlled both these checkpoints and could have made a lot of money if he had not been so honest! Other border guards had been known to become exceedingly rich doing this job.

Pao-Ma Shan: Racehorse Mountain

On the fifth of May, there was an annual horse race held on Pao Ma Shan (Racehorse Mountain). The horses ran from outside East Gate on the right side of the street up that mountain. This was an exceptionally steep, rocky, and difficult route, not only for the horses but also for the riders. At certain points, the riders must dismount and literally crawl up the mountain because it was impossible for both horse and rider to stay the course. The distance from the bottom to the top was not that far, but it took about three to four hours to climb it. The aim was to reach the Buddhist lamasery, surrounded by *wa* (birch) trees at the top of the mountain. Those who wanted to participate had to register with Mr. Yin who himself had also registered his own horse called YinBa (Winner) for the race. Mr. Yin asked me why we did not enter our Old Dragon King. I told him that my father had taken Bei-Yuin out. Our mafu, horse trainer, told me long ago Old Dragon, ridden by Baba's secretary, Yeh SaoScee, and YinBa did race against each other; and YinBa was left far behind. Later, I asked Yeh SaoSceee how fast old Dragon really was and how much he was worth if someone was to buy him.

"All right, I will tell you. You take one thousand silver pins [one pin equals one hundred and fifty ounces], and still, you will not be able to buy him. He is handsome and calm, unlike YinBa who is extremely spirited and rushes forth as soon as he is mounted. Old Dragon King, on the other hand, starts slowly but increases speed as the race progresses so that halfway through the race he looks as if he is flying. YinBa had raced and won against Chase the Wind, which was another very fast horse, so he thought he could easily beat Old Dragon, who was older, smaller, and seemed so gentle and quiet.

"Our Old Dragon King," continued the mafu, "when he is running his fastest, looks as if he is flying, like an arrow piercing the air. His hooves are so fast that they were hardly visible, and yet he is absolutely steady so that the rider could carry a bowl of water without spilling a single drop. That is the kind of horse he is, young master," he concluded, swelling with pride.

Then Yeh SaoScee told the mafu, "Take care of your Old Dragon because Tsen ShouTsee, the provincial garrison commander and Baba's superior, still wanted to race his Chase the Wind against your Dragon King, at least one time." However, on the date of the race, Tsen ShouTsee had not yet returned from Beijing, so both critical horses did not enter the race, and through default, YinBa won; but everyone felt it was an unsatisfactory race.

Children's Battle—Fire on Pao-Ma Shan

The children of the town were separated: the local, Tibetan/ Khamba, on the one hand, and the Han Chinese, on the other. They were antagonistic toward each other at the best of times and were always teasing and bullying and fighting each other under "normal" circumstances. One day, while I was out with two of my friends, some of the "local" boys saw that we were only three and outnumbered, so they began to tease us and throw stones and taunt us. One of older cousin brothers of my friends, about sixteen years of age, saw that we were surrounded and came to our rescue. The little ones saw the bigger and stronger boys approach and started to run away. Their Tibetan friends rushed over to help them, and at the same time, more of our friends joined in the fight too. The local boys began to run, and we gave chase. They ran up the Pao-Ma Shan, and we followed. It was a "children's battle." But no matter how we tried, we could not overtake these boys up the mountain. They had the high ground and began to throw and roll stones and large rocks at us. My friend's cousin shouted to me that I should get my pocket money and pay the boys to get the real ruffians. I offered one silver dollar for each captive. Meanwhile, our opponents climbed higher and higher and continued to roll stones down at us.

"Increase the offer," shouted my friend's cousin, so I raised the ransom to five silver dollars for each captive. The cousin took off his shirt and wrapped it around his head to ward off the stones and urged our "troops" forward. Suddenly, a stone struck my best friend's forehead, and blood spurted out. I put my handkerchief around his head and carried him to Tung BeiBei's house. Tung BeiBei, who was also the "finance" minister of our little town, took one look at my friend and shook his head.

"Silly boys," he muttered. He then applied some *chi li san* to stop the bleeding and told me to go. I saw that my friend was in good hands and rushed out again, shouting to my fellow warriors, "Stop the fighting. I know how to finish those boys and get them down. We will use fire! If Chu Kuo Kung Ming used fire to deflect his enemies, so can we. The hillside is full of trees and dried leaves. One match and the whole mountain will catch on fire."

"You are truly the second ChuKo Kung Ming," said my second friend.

"Then we will see where they can run," I concluded. Once the fire was lit, indeed, the entire mountainside caught on fire with one whoosh. Then we became terrified and ran down the mountain. The fire, meanwhile, rose up the mountainside higher and higher and threatened the lamasery on the top. All the lamas, more than one hundred of them, came out and cut the surrounding birches and used all their drinking water supply to drench the cut trees to form a fire barrier. The fire continued to burn for over an hour and finally died out. The local children, meanwhile, had quietly and simply sneaked around the back side of the mountain and ran home before they were caught. Next day, the Khanding District government posted an announcement, saying that they were going to arrest the boys who set the fire. Mma heard about this and shut me at home until school opened in six weeks. I was under "house arrest" during all that time.

I learned another unforgettable power of nature—first, was the earthquakes and now fire: neither was to be scoffed at or played with. I was kept indoors for several days till the furor had died down.

Rev. Len Hai on Pao-Ma Shan

My mother had heard that a Chinese monk from Chengdu was in the lamasery on Pao-Ma Shan to learn Tibetan scriptures because he was planning to go to Tibet to become a lama. I was curious and decided to go and visit this monk. Our neighbor, Song Lama's elder brother, was preparing to go to that lamasery to discuss some scriptures with the monk and asked me if I wanted to go with him as he knew I liked to climb mountains. I immediately agreed and said that I was also interested in meeting that monk. Early one morning, we set off and started to climb, but we were barely halfway up when I heard him call me, "Ahya, oh je je, oh ja ja [Oh, dear, dear, how hot I am]." I looked back in surprise.

"It is not so hot. How come you feel so hot?" I asked.

"You are but a child, I am an old man. I cannot go up a mountain so fast." He then took off the upper half of his garments and tied it around his waist.

The *khanzan* or Khamba's adult clothing was an all-purpose garment. It was a sort of a coat with two large brass buttons on the left used only when needed. These "coats" were very long, very large and voluminous, and made of sheepskin with the fur facing inside. The length of the garment went from head to toe. During the day, it was pulled up to the knee, and the extra length was tied around the waist with a thick rope made of leather or hemp, which also served as a "tool" when needed. At night, this "belt" was unfastened, and the garment became a wraparound blanket, thus allowing the wearer to bed down anywhere on the ground. Thus, if you were traveling, you should not be surprised if early one morning someone emerged out of the snow or sprang from behind a large rock.

When we arrived at the lamasery, it was already noon. Soong Lama's brother told the gatekeeper lama that we wanted to meet the Chinese monk, and he came to see the *kambu* (abbot) also. While Soong Lama's brother conversed with the Chinese monk and the abbot, the gatekeeper took me to another monk called Len Hui, eating a large bowl of green-black vegetables; and on seeing me, he told me to sit on a large disc and wait until he finished eating his lunch.

"What are you eating?" I asked, full of curiosity.

"This is *yu-tsai* [mustard green]," he answered, not bothering to stop eating.

I said, "When we eat yu-tsai, we usually fry it with green onions and ginger, not boil it like you do."

Then he told me that during his period of meditation, he ate only one meal a day, which can only be boiled without oil, salt, or any kind of seasoning. I thought to myself, *how good could that be?* I decided that to be a monk was not easy.

"What is your name?" he asked. I told him my father's name and situation.

71

"My mother came from a Tung Sa Tang [a Buddhist sect] and it was she who had told me about you and that you have some occult and supernatural powers."

"Ha-ha-ha!" He laughed heartily. "What supernatural powers? I can hardly know myself. People must have made some mistake. In Tibet, such lamas do exist, but one must know the Pali language to understand what those lamas are saying. Many of the Tibetan scriptures were translated from Pali, so to really understand Buddhism, one must know Pali or Tibetan.

"What are you studying?" he asked me.

"Chinese," I told him.

He said that it was good to study Chinese but advised that I should not forget the local language and that I should continue to study it also. Now, eighty plus years later, I have left Tibetan far behind; aside from a few common sentences and words of greetings, I am no longer fluent in my first language. I am ashamed and must apologize to Len Hui Lama for not following his advice.

Later, I learned that he did reach Lhasa and, after three years of intensive studies, had acquired the title of Iron-Rod Lama with full occult powers. I also learned, when I was in India, that Chairman Mao Tse Tung had invited him to China. I always wondered about the outcome of that meeting.

Lumber Raft from GoDa Mountain

GoDa Mountain was East Lucheng/Khanding. This mountain was extremely steep, one had to almost get to a supine position to see the peak:

Mountain rises from one's face

Like from hoof of horses to their ears

A vertical wall.

Behind this wall-like mountain, the landscape was completely different. It was all forested with cypress, juniper, and all kinds of other trees. From here, many trees were felled and slid down the mountainside into the roaring river to collect near the Eastern Gate of Lucheng, where an enormous "log platform" was formed. It was said that soaking the timber in water allows logs to dry without cracking, and lumber, which had undergone such a soaking, was stronger and longer lasting. I was very intrigued with this huge "raft" and often took my dog, Laischee, to play "on it" without knowing the extreme danger my dog and I were in. Later, when I was in India, I was talking to the principal of the boys' school, St. Joseph's College in Darjeeling and was telling him about the "lumber raft." He said that it reminded him of his home in Canada and how extremely dangerous it was to 'play' on them, my dog and I could have been easily crushed between those moving logs,

At the time of ChuKuo KungMing and the Warring States, the armies needed arrows, so KungMing sent General Go to the forests of Lucheng to cut down the trees and manufacture arrows. Therefore, Lucheng's was also called TaJieng Lu, meaning Arrow-Making Lu, or DaJieng Lu in Tibetan. I believe it is still used by some of the older folks to this day.

There was another small mountain called TseUr Po (Small Slope) situated north of Lucheng. It was not as difficult to climb as Paow-Ma Shan nor as steep, noble, and imposing as GoDa Mountain; but all the political, educational, economic, and religious institutions were situated at the base of TseUr Po. For instance, our school, the girls' school; the government offices, all the traders from SanSchee; and the army corps were there. The Ming Tsen Tu Schee (i.e., the local Khamba government) was located there. The Inland Christian Church, the Catholic Church, and the SsaCha Monastery (Sa Ja Gomba), which was the largest Red Hat Sect of Buddhist Monastery, were all located there. It was an area of bustling import and export commerce. All these activities were located here because Tse Ur Po was neither steep nor high, the roads were wide, and there was a very large level expanse around which shops and small eating places were located. Children, like me, liked to ride their horse through the streets because it was level and wide. People liked to stroll through these streets in the evenings or climb up the "small slope" and generally greet and socialize with one another.

End of the Ming Tseng TuScee Line

I used to know two brothers, Jia NiengKo and Jia NiengFon, who had a large walled garden at the back of their house. There were several kinds of fruit trees, and it was a very quiet place because hardly anyone came there. It was a perfect place for my friends and I to go and study for our exams there. One day some fellow students and I climbed over the wall into this garden for this very specific purpose: there was a kind of fruit called *hwa-hung*, very much like a small apple but with a sweet and tart taste. Our horses loved them too, so I used to pick some for myself and some for my horse. We often did this especially during exam time. Alas, that day, we were discovered by the owners, so they set their huge mastiff at us. A Tibetan mastiff—or lion dog, as the locals called them—is extremely fierce and bred to protect their owners and kill intruders. At the Big Grassland, the sheep and yak herders often collected their herds of animals in separate groups, each guarded by its own mastiff. Sometimes thieves would try to steal a head of cattle or a sheep; but often they would be found the next day with a lion dog standing over them, having their necks broken or bitten to death, or at the least badly mauled. This was the Tibetans' best and most-feared guard. There we were, frozen to the spot by a lion dog with a huge white head, brown feet, and black body. He blocked our exit, and we were trapped. We offered money to the servant to call off the beast, but he only laughed at us and refused. As we were arguing with him, a gentleman appeared and asked, "What is the meaning of this? What are you boys doing here?"

"Please, sir, we are San SenScee students, and because of the exams, we were looking for a quiet place to study and revise and found your garden to be the ideal." Seeing that we did have bundles of books under our arms, he told the servant to lead the dog away, adding that Number One Son had returned and to go and see to him. Then I asked, 'That Number One Son—is he called Jia NiengKo?"

"Do you know him?" the gentleman asked.

"We met at Dr. Anderson's house," I replied.

"Then you know Dr. Anderson?"

"Yes, we often went to Mr. Koo's for tennis and often met there."

He was very pleased and asked me to go and see Dr. An. At first, I did not know to whom he referred to as Dr. An, then I realized that 'Westerners' often shortened the names of people with long ones; our own names usually had only one syllable.

"Come with me. He is here."

I asked him if he could allow my school friends to come with us. He replied that if they also knew Dr. An, then they too could come. Only Wong YuanHong knew Dr. An, and he did not want to come, so I went alone with the gentleman to see Dr. An. When we arrived in their living room, there was no one there; but turning toward the front garden, I saw a large group of people standing in front of a large tent. I saw Dr. Anderson carrying a medical bag with a very angry expression on his face and exclaiming, "He is already dead. How can you expect me to bring him back to life? I do not have that kind of magic!" He turned and saw me in the crowd and said to me, "He was already dead before he even came into town. His breath had already left." Sonsaying, he took his bag and strode away.

Everyone burst into tears. All at once, we heard loud wailing come from within the house, and we learned that the younger brother too had just died mysteriously. Mr. Ming TsenJia had no more descendants because neither brother had married. Sad it was indeed. Quietly, as I left the house, I could hear the terrible moaning and crying of the family especially that of the mother.

Soong Lama

We had to move again, this time from Nan Meng Street to a house on SanScee Street. In the middle of the living room was a large stone, which jutted fifteen inches through the floorboards. We tried to dig it up but found it was impossible because the buried portion was even larger than the exposed one. We would have had to tear up the entire house to do so. It was like a stone iceberg, of which 90 percent of its total size was submerged. Baba said that since we cannot budge it, we should cover it with a nice piece of cloth to make it more presentable. But Mma was Buddhist. She saw this as something auspicious and thought it was not proper to cover it up or touch it in any way. I was sent to fetch a certain Tibetan Lama named Soong to come and advise us as to what to do.

I was not certain about the real name of Soong Lama because Tibetans used their given names as their family names also, and only Chinese attached a surname to their given names. But here was a Tibetan lama who used a Chinese surname for his name. When Soong Lama came to Lucheng/Khanding), no one asked because no one seemed interested, least of all himself. All he was concerned with was that people believed in his healing powers and paid him for his services. At first, he lived at the base of the TseUr Po; but later, he moved into own his house, which he had built himself, at the foothills of Paow-Ma Shan—opposite our house. Soong Lama had a deep red mark the size of an egg yolk on the middle of his forehead, between his eyes; and this made him look like a holy man. When people encountered him on the streets, they would kowtow or prostrate themselves before him. I remember when someone was sick, he would pray and splatter some "holy" water on that person, but if the person was seriously ill, then he would use his spit! I did not like this at all, but those patients seemed to recover. Soong Lama had set up his treatment "shop" in his little house and was seeing patients, vetted by his own elder brother, Jia Chiang. This brother was also a lama, but he did not possess the spiritual powers of a healer, so his job was to receive and vet the patients coming to see Soong Lama. I was already very familiar with both the lamas, so I went directly into Soong Lama's treatment room. I was surprised to see Jia Chiang's wife there.

"Aja Chiang aunty, what are you doing here?" I exclaimed.

"I'm not feeling well, so I asked Master to help me."

Then Soong Lama entered and saw me. He turned and asked his brother, "Se Ku Cho [Golden Prince, as some used to call me] has come. Why did you not tell me?"

I interjected, "It is my fault. I wanted to come directly to you and ask you to come home."

"What is the matter at your home?" asked Soong Lama.

"You see, there is a large stone in our living room, and we cannot dig it out, but we want to know if we can use anything to cover it."

Then I added irrelevantly, "Also, my stomach often hurts, and my sister's head hurts too. Her room is in the far end of the house, and she is not often allowed to go out." I just wanted to "test" Soong Lama, because somehow, I had always suspected his sincerity. What boyish audacity to test such a revered lama. "So please, Master, come and say some prayer for us and advise us as to what to do," I concluded.

"I will come with you at once," he responded.

"What about Aja? Will you take care of her first?" I asked.

"She can wait here."

Soong Lama and I walked home together. When we approached our house and saw my mother, he remarked to her, "So you have a big stone in your living room?"

"Yes," answered Mma, surprised, not knowing that I had already told him about it.

"You must never touch that stone," said Soong Lama.

"My son often has stomach aches, and my daughter's head often hurts," added Mma.

"That's because you have disturbed that stone," he exclaimed, somewhat worried; then he sat on a low stool with his eyes closed and mumbled some prayers. After a while, he opened his eyes and said, "Bring me a piece of red silk brocade." He took the cloth we gave him and covered the stone and chanted, "Ohm mani peh meh hum [Hail to the jewel in the lotus]" several times.

(NB: If one really wanted to understand the true and full meaning of these words, one must find a good learned lama to be one's teacher. Still, it would take him three months to explain them.)

Then he took his rosary and placed them on my sister's and my head, said a few words, and proclaimed, "Good. Everything will be all right now." Mma then took ten silver yuans and gave them to him. He smiled, took them, and put them into his pocket and left.

Later, I told Mma, "My stomach never hurt, nor did *jiehjieh's* [elder sister] head hurt. Those silver yuans were wasted."

"Do not be so rude. Do not disrespect your elders," said Mma, but she never again consulted Soong Lama. Her superstition was broken.

Peas Tsampa

The staple food of the Khampas/Khantsan and Tibetan people was tsampa, which is still widely consumed today. It is a stiff porridge made of ground barley, mixed with vegetable oil or yak butter, and rolled into size of golf balls and deep-fried. They were consumed with Tibetan tea, and when traveling, they were wrapped in cloth and eaten en route, making them a very portable snack. The best tsampa was made of oats, barley, or peas. The peas were the cheapest and were bought and eaten only by the horsekeepers and the poorest country folks known as *ooh-la-wa* people. It was customary for these poorest-of-the poor Tibetans to round up other peoples' horses or cows to pasture or barn in exchange for a few balls of peas tsampa. They also performed any menial job for those who needed them, and yet, they were disliked and despised for their pains. This custom dated back to the Ching dynasty and is one small example among numerous reasons for the antagonism between the Chinese and the Tibetans. Once my father rewarded an ooh-la-wa sixty pieces of gold for something he had done for Baba, this poor wretch was at first more suspicious and astonished than grateful because he had never known such kindness from anyone.

There was a merchant called Lee ChenPao from Chengdu who owned a business in Lucheng. It was a variety store and sold items such as needle and thread, dry goods, small tools, and anything anyone needed. He was a thorough shopkeeper. He could speak the local dialect, Tibetan and Chinese. He conversed with the well-off customers and talked to the horse keepers and even the ooh-la-was. Everyone liked him. He was congenial and generous, sometimes even roasted a goat or cow and shared the meat with all his customers. We called him Chhomoben-la (big proprietor). But for himself, he was very frugal and ate like those ooh-la-wa. He even carried with him the peas tsampas, which he ate with water instead of tea. Baba felt sorry for him and often invited him to eat with us and chatted with him. When Baba was being transferred from Dawu to Lucheng, Lee ChenPow asked Baba if he could travel with us because it was not too safe to travel alone. We set up camp outside a village called Tailing, which was famous for its lion dogs. Lee ChenPow shared a tent with Baba. Suddenly, there was a loud sound like a muffled distant thunder. Both the other two occupants were startled and quickly clapped their hands to their noses and guffawed with laughter.

Baba, whose cot was further removed from the other three, asked, "What happened?"

Lee ChenPow came over to Baba, trembling with fright, and confessed, stammering, "I'm sorry, your lordship, I just … I just … without manners, farted. And they all laughed at me. I am sorry to disturb your sleep."

"Never mind," said Baba. "It is because you ate something, and it is not digested."

"I did not eat anything odd, only peas tsampa, what I always eat."

"Ahhh, then it is understandable. Peas tsampa is very difficult to digest. Eaten in small quantities, there is no problem, but in large amounts, it is difficult." Lee ChenPow then shook his head and said, "Living out on the grasslands, every penny not spent is a penny saved. I cannot afford anything else."

Baba was very sympathetic toward him and always looked out for him and often shared his meal with him. The others called Lee ChenPow "one shot to heaven."

Later, my friend Yang MaTsan said to me, "He farts once and reached your father. Isn't it one shot to heaven? Then he laughed till his side ached.

When Baba arrived in Lucheng, Gov. Cheng HsiaNing had not yet arrived; in fact, he was not coming and was being replaced by Liu YuJue, a rather short and plump Buddhist who seemed to be full of good nature. On the first day, he went to the SooJa Temple to worship. He also believed in lamas and asked them to meditate and bring him good luck. Their method was rather different from any I had ever seen: a white silk scarf called *khada* was wound around the neck of one of the lamas, then two others pulled on either end of the scarf until the lama almost fainted! Suddenly, the lama with the silk around his neck jumped up with a loud yell, "Ahya, Goong ju soong [Dear god]." This was the time people could ask him to tell their fortunes or ask him questions of special interests. Gov. Liu YuJue had also brought two Chinese monks along with him, one called Ta Yung FaScee and the other Ta Kung FaScee, so our new governor had both the old and new holy men from whom to request good fortune.

Chapter 4

FATHER TRANSFERRED TO LUDING AS DISTRICT COMMISSIONER

We had not been in Lucheng long when Baba was transferred again, this time as the district commissioner of Luding. Since this was only twenty li from Lucheng, Baba decided not to make the entire family move again, seeing that we had only just moved and settled.

Lucheng was famous for its cable bridge over the Tadu River. This bridge was suspended on a pair of large steel cables, and the main section of the bridge was surfaced with wooden planks. Though it was only about three quarters of a mile long, it was extremely high—about a third of a mile, 1,760 feet, above the rushing, tumbling waters. Seven cables were wound together to make up to the thickness of a man's arm, stretched from one bank to the other; and on either side of the bridge, it was further strengthened by a pair of even thicker cables. Small chains hung from the stout cable rails to form the handrails. On top of the seven cables, boards were placed with one-inch gaps in between to allow wind to pass through, thus diminishing the danger of the boards being lifted up by the strong prevailing winds in the district. The entire bridge was secured directly into the mountainside. It was the most difficult and frightening bridge to cross, as it tended not only to sway from side to side but also undulate up and down as one walked. Though I was able to run along our "wave bridge" in school, this *real* wave bridge was terrifying: the practice I had on our pretend wave bridge was of little help. I remember there were times when I stayed at Luding Bridge for a couple of nights to meet up with friends without crossing it. While Baba was in Lucheng, he wanted to leave his political career and go into business. The Manchu government was becoming less and less popular, and the people were getting more and more restless and discontented. My father's situation, though he was well liked and respected, was getting more and more tenuous. He discussed this with Lui ChenPao that he wanted to go into the "buying and selling" business. He would buy dried goods in LuCheng, such as soya sauce, Sichuan wine, silk brocade, quilts, dried barley, peas, etc., and sell them in ChengDu. It was decided, so all the goods were stored in a warehouse and were sold after the New Year. But all the money Baba made was used up, and he was not happy. He discussed his situation with his old friend, the finance minister, and his brother. "If we continue like this in Lucheng, going back and forth between Lucheng and Chengdu with our merchandise, we might as well live in Chengdu and try our luck there." The old finance minister said, "You have done well for the government and made our countryside safe and orderly, and yet, you do not even have a head of cattle to your name. I heard that your batman has built a house and owns a cattle farm in Dawu. Where did he get that money? He must have used his position 'well,' eh, eh, eh?" "Ahya, sir, Elder Brother," addressing his brother, "our family has been the protectors of the border states since the times of Emperor Han Fung, and we were awarded the black flag as our family color. When we arrived in a troubled area with our black flags flying, the people knew they would be safe and protected. We understood and empathized with the peoples of this region. Conditions were difficult and poor. Often the people had neither food nor clothing and had to live as ooh-la-wa, but we took care of them and considered it our greatest responsibilities. The previous Ching dynasty never cared about the lives of these people, and this new government of ours seems to be similarly heartless and uncaring. We have been the protectors of these areas for the past four centuries, so I deeply understand this kind of dishonest behavior. It is too easy to bribe and extort the poor and dispossessed. When I came to this post, I had vowed that I would never become corrupt and will do as much as I could to help these people, and I have. I never asked for any favors from anyone above me and never extracted bribes from those below me. I never pursued fame or fortune. I wanted no regrets and no guilt from my actions. But nowadays, many new 'capable' workers have come, and I think I should retire from politics and become a businessman. Unfortunately, half a century has passed in one blink of an eye. My situation cannot be blamed on anyone. Only I am to be blamed. Sometimes I did not make the right choice. We cannot help but leave this place and start a new life." This was the longest speech I had ever heard from my father, and I was proud of him. I understood all what Baba said, even when he spoke about the "new capable people," implying that maybe he was not "capable," therefore humbling himself. Our forebears had survived the Warring States era, and he himself had taken the last imperial examination of the Ching dynasty. He went through the Sun Yat-Sun Revolution and passed the College of Law and the examinations of magistrates and became a state councilor and finally judge. He became the district commissioner and the judge of numerous districts. He was in charge of tax collection, but being a thoroughly honest government official, a rare occurrence, he ended up with "two empty sleeves." Now finally, he must sadly say good-bye to the region he had live for half his life and the place where I was born and spent the first few years of my life. Before we left, I went with my schoolmates, Hwa ChungJuin and KouChang, to the photographic shop to take a photo of us. When it was printed, I asked Hwa DaGe (Big Brother) to write a couple on it for us:

"Arrows shoot the flying swan, riding horses singing parting songs.

These are tragic actions just as day and night are separating at dawn and dust.

Friends too are separating."

So saying, we three went to the base of Mount DaJien to comfort one another and to wish that we might meet again someday. (A few years later, when the Communists had swept through the land, they were also in Chengdu. They had ordered Kou Chang, who had suffered from vertigo, to climb up a tree to cut firewood; unfortunately, he fell, broke his neck, and died. ChungJuin carried his brother's body to the Communist camp, but the prison guard there 'misunderstood' the situation and put ChungJuin in prison, where he remained for ten years without trial. Later, he jumped into the Lucheng River and drowned. I have since lost that photograph during one of our many moves. Oftentimes, even up till today, when I think of my childhood, I weep with boundless sorrow.

Farewell to Half a Century: Road from Lucheng to Chengdu

We had a dozen or so "running/walking" horses, i.e., good horses that could walk long distances and run short races, but my father thought we had too many. When we arrived in Lucheng, he gave away a few and sold a few. We kept Bei-Yuin, the Old Dragon King, until he died and left only a chestnut, which Baba rode. This was a good walker and racer and was his favorite, but when we left Lucheng, he even gave him away to Wah DaGe. He only kept a small yearling for me to ride from Lucheng to Chengdu. I fed him myself, took him to the river daily to water, and groom him and took him for a daily run out of the city gate. I was very fond of him. Early one morning, in the spring of 1924, we decided to leave Lucheng. Baba called for the palanquins for himself, Mma, DaJieh (my elder sister), and Shan Jieh (my third cousin sister). I led my horse while our servant girl and servant from Shan Schee Street walked behind. I saw my two sworn brothers, ChungJuin and Kouchang; my sister's best friend, Nan; and her elder sister with her two-year-old boy, Liner, come toward us. We all embraced and cried. I comforted Nan Jiehjieh, saying, "Does not your family have a house in Chengdu? So you will be going home. Then we will be together again." She cried even more and said, "Where do I have a home in Chengdu? My mother and father died long ago. I have no brother and sister. I have no home there anymore. Ahya, Ahya."

"All right, all right," I said awkwardly and pulled my hand away from Nan Jiehjieh and told my sister to climb into the palanquin.

All our friends walked with us out of the East Gate, over the Middle Bridge, and past Bee Hive Street; then nearing the big bend on the street, Baba called, "Enough. Stop." He stepped down from the palanquin and proclaimed to Wah ChungJuin and Kou Chang, "You can see us off a thousand li, but we must eventually part."

"Take my farewell greetings to your family." Then he raised his hands over his head, one fist within the other, in the traditional Chinese greeting. ChangJuin stood apart while I ran toward him, trembling all over, and said, "I hope we meet again." "Okay, okay, okay, of course, of course," he replied, not knowing where to look. And I thought, *Farewell to ChungJuin. Farewell to Tse Ur Po. If I were to see all these friends and this place again, it will only be in my dreams.* Meanwhile, BeiFu and Small Auntie caught up to our servant girl. It was quite an entourage.

It was extremely difficult for my pony to pass Big Bend because the mountain path was treacherously narrow and stony, and many a rider and man had slipped and fallen to their deaths; thus, this section of the road was commonly known as the ten-thousand-men ditch. I dismounted my pony and led him by the reins, carefully avoiding the larger slippery stones as much as possible. "Why do you take him by the reins instead of riding him?" asked BeiFu from behind.

"Because he is a young horse and not used to this stony path. He may slip. If I rode him and he slipped, we both will fall into that ditch and join those skeletons! It is safer to take him by the reins," I explained, slightly annoyed at my uncle. We arrived at LuJi, a hamlet of only a few dwellings. At the gate of one of these homes, there was a paper lantern hung outside the door, and on it was written:

Stay here before it gets dark

Rise and leave before the cock crows.

I realized that this was a small inn—too small. How could it accommodate our large party? What about my little horse? My father had already arranged for everyone to stay for the night. He told Yang Kwangdai (also known as Yang Cheng, his batman) to take the little horse to the backyard and check if there was a back door and to stand guard there against wild animals. Somehow we all managed to get some sleep somewhere in this tiny inn and peacefully spent the night. BeiFu told Baba that I never did ride the horse because it was not used to the rocky path and that I had made him very nervous holding the horse by the reins: one step, one slide, one step, one slide, My father decided to lead the pony himself and told me to go into the palanquin with all the women. I was very unhappy about this, but I had no choice. When we reached Luding Bridge, I was terrified for my horse, but Yang Tsancheng said that he would cross without any difficulty, and he was right. Somehow the little horse was able to avoid all the spaces between the boards on the bridge. Since Baba had been posted in Luding/Lucheng before, the border guards came to escort us through the big mountain forest, Ta Shen-Ning and Hsiao Shen-Ning (Big Forest and Small Forest), because it was a place known for bandits who could easily hide among the dense forests and ambush unwary travelers. The leader of the border police insisted on escorting us. He offered to take my little horse off our hands and save us the trouble of crossing the bridge with him. I disliked this man instantly. The more he praised my little pony, the more I did not like him. But I began to believe him and asked Yang TsanCheng if my horse was really that good. Yang TsanCheng, an honest man from Hunan, with a hot temper said angrily, "Of course, it is a good horse, but that man not only got your horse, but he has his meals plus the twenty silver pieces your father gave him. Hrump!"

Then the leader said that we had reached around the mountain, and they now had to take my father's leave. We had been walking for seven days and finally arrived at Neetou where we booked ourselves into a hotel. We had crossed two mountains and two rivers, and we were all exhausted, so Baba and BeiFu decided that we should rest for one day before proceeding. I was happy that my horse was returned to me.

Rest at Ling Tsing District for a Day

Neetou, in the district of Ling Tsing, was the town where my last tutor had come from. It was a much larger and busier town than Khangding. The streets were wider and crowded with people going about their business or shopping. When we were settled in the hotel, Baba took me to visit my last tutor, Chang Furu *LaoScee*. I kowtowed to him, as was the custom, and he returned my obeisance and said, "You were my last student because when I returned to my hometown, I did not take any more students. I did not want to teach anymore." Then turning to my father, he continued, "I understand why you left LuCheng. To remain there will be a dead end for you. There are no opportunities for the likes of us in our rapidly changing world. The days of our empire are dying, the Empress Dowager is losing her power and control over the eunics day by day. The common people's clamor for a republic under the call of Dr. Sun Yat-Sun is getting stronger. It is good you are leaving."

I looked at him closely and saw the increased wrinkles on his face. His back was slightly bent, and behind his thick eyeglasses, tears began to flow.

Baba said, "Old brother, why be so sad? At least we can say we did not waste our time."

"Ten years on the West River … ten years on the East River—how can you say we are finished?"

He smiled a bit after Baba's words and looked at me. Pointing, he said to me, "Do not play all day. You must put your entire mind on the books. I have two sentences to advise you: Hard work results in success. Play all day results in nothing."

This was a gift from teacher to pupil. "Remember this always." So saying, he began to weep. I was always rather afraid of him, but today I felt exceedingly close to him. I never saw him again, but even until today, I have remembered his two sentences and the tears behind his thick lens and felt very sorry for the sadness in him I never understood.

A Poetic Innkeeper

After leaving Lucheng fourteen days ago with fourteen stops in between, we finally arrived at Yungcheng (or Rongcheng. This town was named after the *ronghwa* (hibiscus) flower because it was growing everywhere. There were many teashops, small restaurants, and other shops selling opium. The three "beverages" served in all these eating places were tea, wine, and opium, mostly opium. Most of the customers were coolies and palanquin bearers. When we had settled ourselves into a small inn, I saw our bearers rush into an inn and borrow two wooden planks from the door of the restaurant. (The doors were made up of planks slid into metal runners on the floor and the overhead lintels to fill up the door space. To open the door, the planks were slid out and propped up on sawhorses used as benches in the restaurants.) Our bearer took the two planks to a small empty area beside the outhouse, and from his inner pocket, he took out his black bowl and a small long pouch out of which he took out a small lamp and pipe. Then he lay down on the plank and began to smoke. Within minutes, he was lost to this world. I was so astonished and ran to call my sisters, "Mind your own business and stop being so inquisitive." I was irritated and went to Yang KuanDai to tell him. He told me, "They are all like that. Smoking is more important than food to them." He then took me to a small teahouse to look at the couplet outside the restaurant. Inside, there were two tables seating at the most six diners at each; on the left, there was a stove with only one burner. On the doorway, in front of the burner, was this couplet:

"Busy for name, busy for profit, amid the turmoil steal some leisure.

Have a cup of tea. Hard to live, hard to die,

Capture a moment in between for a glass of wine."

Baba came up to me and asked, "So son, what do you think of it?"

"I think it is good."

"How good? What exactly do you mean?"

Before I could answer, BeiFu said, "That man who wrote it must be someone who is not only cultured and educated but also must have known some bitterness in his life. Pity we do not have time to go and converse with him."

Then Baba said, "In all this half of my lifetime, I have traveled in many parts and have met many high officials and important people. I have never come across such a fine couplet in such a lowly place—a couplet so profound and yet so exquisitely simple."

Older Cousin Sister Marry

We finally arrived in a town called Chiungzhou and found ourselves in a rather dignified hotel. We took a large suite comprised of several rooms. We entered the suite, which had a large sitting room in the middle. To the east of this sitting room, BeiFu and his wife and infant stayed while Baba and Mma took the room in the west. My older cousin sister and my sister stayed in the room next to BeiFu while I stayed in a little room next to my parents. We commonly used the two small side doors on either side of the sitting room, but there was a large door in the center of the back wall of the sitting room, which was never opened. If we needed anything, we asked the manager to send for it. The servants were called *hoji* or *yowscee*, and since I had never heard these names before, I wanted to shout out and "practice," but I was afraid Baba would not be pleased. When we were still settling in, a hoji appeared with a box of *dian-xin* (small edibles) and tea. BeiFu came out of his room, the hoji quickly bowed to him, and he did the same when Baba emerged from his room. It was not a hoji at all but a relative. Mma told me to salute Fan Elder Brother and also told me that he was to be my elder brother-in-law. Fan took my hands and said, "Do you not remember me? We met at Lucheng." Then I remembered that he was working at some government office at the South Gate area. What I really remembered was that my dog had bitten a vendor who was selling onion cakes, and during the struggle, some of those cakes fell on the ground. The vendor caught me and demanded that I pay for those cakes. During that argument, because the vendor was trying to hit my dog with a stick, Fan Elder Brother saw us and told the vendor to calm down and picked up his cakes and paid him. I never realized that this young man was to be my brother-in-law. This same Fan Elder Brother now put the boxes of food he was carrying on the table in the middle of the sitting room and asked us to eat after our long journey. I called my sisters to come out, but only Jiehjieh did so. DaJieh would not. She was crying. "Fourth Brother, you go ahead and eat. I am not hungry. Don't feel like eating." Then I told the rest of the family at the table, "I don't know why she is crying. I only told her to come out soon or the food will get cold. She said that she was not hungry and did not want to eat."

"Okay," said Small Auntie, "if she is not hungry and does not want to eat, then let us not wait. The food is getting cold."

BeiFu wiped his eyes and looked down. Baba looked stern, and even Third Sister seemed ponderous. I did not know what was going on, so I filled my bowl with rice and put some side dishes on top.

Mma asked me, "What are you doing, ChiPei?"

"This is for DaJieh in case she gets hungry later," I replied.

"All right, all right, all right," said Mma with a small smile and a nod.

Then Small Auntie announced sarcastically, "A good brother, hrrm. If you loved your little sister and hugged her a little, she will cry less."

Small Auntie's baby cried a lot; and I did not like her runny nose, her arms and legs all flailing about. Small Auntie knew that I disliked this kind of action and took every opportunity to tease me. I tried to ignore her and not lose my temper, but on occasions I did. Once, I was taunted to such an extent that even BeiFu spoke out in defense of me. "Leave him alone. He is only a small boy and knows no better. He tends to be a bit too upright and fair, but you should give him some allowance."

I had already given in to Small Auntie and ran away from her. Mma always supported Big Sister because she did not have a mother of her own to support her. At around nine that night, Fan Big Brother came again, talked to BeiFu, and spoke to Baba. Big Sister came out of her room and knelt before BeiFu and cried, "*Dieh*," (father).

BeiFu pulled her up, tears flowing down his face. Words could not come out. I felt very bad because, at last, I understood the reason of the tension in that room all afternoon.

(In those days, being "married off" was often a very frightening prospect because, more often than not, the couple involved would never have met each other. They were unions of rich families or of economic convenience among the less well-off, as was the case for my DaJieh, or simply because the two fathers were very good friends, as was the case for me. I was to marry my father's best friend's first daughter when we came of age. (Of course, this never came about because of World War II when families, villages, towns, and cities were torn asunder.)

That was why Big Sister and her father were weeping so heartbreakingly; neither family had known each other. Fan Big Brother had seen her in the marketplace and had taken a liking for her. He had also noticed the family she was always with and how diligently she worked and her filial piety for her own father and her uncle. Then he had approached Uncle and proposed marriage to his daughter.

Baba very seriously addressed Big Sister, "Jin Kuan, listen to your third uncle [my Baba]. The Fan family is a good and honest country family. Show your filial piety to your father- and mother-in-law and take care of your new sisters- and brothers-in-law. Your mother died when you were only a small child, so your third uncle and auntie [my father and mother] took care of you just as if you had been their very own so that other people will not look down on you. Now I am asking your fourth brother [me] to accompany you to the Fans' house. This is an extremely simple marriage. Due to your father's and my circumstances, this is the only thing we can do." Baba's voice faltered, and he took out his handkerchief and wiped his eyes. Mma and my sister silently wept continuously. My heart was all in confusion.

Then Small Auntie shouted, "Enough. What else is there to say? All these tears, the carriage has been waiting for a long time."

Suddenly, Big Sister came over to Small Auntie and kowtowed before to her and cried, "Please, look after my father well."

Small Auntie said, "All right, if I don't look after that old man, who will, eh, eh? Stop this crying and go. Go quickly."

Big Sister—shoulders shaking with her sobs, tears streaming down her cheeks—went to the palanquin; she climbed in, calling once more, "Dieh."

BeiFu slumped into a chair and let out a long sigh. Then Yan KuanTai, taking a lantern in one hand and me in the other, slowly walked in front of the palanquin.

I asked him, "Do you know where Fan Brother's family live?"

"No, but Fan told me how to get there."

After about half an hour, we reached our destination and saw Fan *Hsien-sen* at the window. He came out. I saw a middle-aged woman, who must have been Mr. Fan's mother, come running out also. She stopped in front of me, looked into the palanquin, and said, "New Person has arrived. Why didn't anyone tell me, Aya, Aya? Prepare everything."

Fan Brother said, "The palanquin has only just arrived. Don't be in such a hurry." He gently helped Big Sister out of the palanquin and led her to the house. Fan Brother said that the house belonged to his relatives, so they would stay there for a few days. Later, he would move to his own family house in the countryside. He invited us to visit them one day. Just as everyone was going in, I quietly slipped the twenty silver yuans to Cousin sister, which Mma had asked me to give to her.

I whispered, "Mma did not want anyone to see this, and since she had no time to buy you a present herself, so please, buy whatever you want yourself."

Big Sister cried again and said, "Fourth Brother, your mother and Third Uncle, and your sister treated me like my own parents would have and made me feel truly like a part of your family. I do not know when I will be able to hold your mother in my arms again." Big Sister became more and more overwrought while I tried to control myself.

Then Fan Brother came out and said, "It is late. Early tomorrow morning, we will come and say good-bye." Except for this tragic and the Juingcheng darkness, I cannot remember anything else of that day.

ShinJing River—Most Difficult River to Cross in the World

It took less than a day to go from Shinjing to Chengdu, which was our final stop. The ShinJin River was not that wide. One could easily see the other side, and the water was not even very deep or swift, but there were three consecutive rivers to cross, and there was only one ferry carrying one palanquin at a time from one bank to the next. Unlike the TaDu River in Luding (Khangding)—which was wide, deep, and rapid—there was a bridge to take people and animals across quickly; but at Shinjin, there were no bridges, and three rivers divided the area into three districts. It normally took three hours to cross all three rivers, plying the ferry back and forth; but because of our large entourage of six palanquins, twenty-six people, plus horses, it took us from dawn until two in the afternoon to get everyone across. So the local people used to say, "You travel on all the roads under heaven. You can hardly cross the Shinjin River."

Chengdu at Last

We had experienced staying in hotels four or five times along our way, but this hotel in Chengdu was different from all the previous ones. When we entered the rather large establishment, there was a counter in the foyer, behind which stood a thin bespectacled man. He was the manager and came toward us, bowed, and offered to help us. My father said that we had seven in our party plus a few servants. He asked us for all our names and how many rooms we required. My father replied that two rooms would be sufficient for the seven of us, plus a small room for our maidservant.

"Yes, yes, we have two such rooms, one with and one without an anteroom," he said. BeiFu took the room without the anteroom, and we took the other. Baba had meant for Yan Tsancheng to stay in the anteroom, but he protested, saying, "There are beds for the servants in the hotel, and I have already reserved them for us, so the servant girl can stay in the anteroom."

BeiFu said, "No wonder Third Lord is so fond of you. You are so efficient and considerate."

"What do you mean considerate? I have served Third Lord and traveled with him for so many years, and he has always treated me like a member of the family." Then turning to Baba, he continued, "Also, I have bought a piece of land in Gokah, near Dawu, where my wife has given birth to a son. I have a few heads of cattle and some horses. I want to bury my old bones there. When I have seen that you and your family are all settled in Chengdu, I will return there." He looked at Baba and quickly left. Baba's eyes followed him out and then went into his own room with a sigh.

We stayed in the hotel for three days; then on the fourth day, Nan *laoscee*, who used to be a teacher of mine, came to meet us in Chengdu, and he had found a house for us. It was near the Jin Hwa Bridge over Jin Ho (river) on Hsuen Ho Street in the new section of the city, Chengdu Saocheng (New City). BeiFu's son, JeeKao, my cousin, was also called ChiMing (like my name ChiPei), the name I was known as when I entered school; and only teachers could address a person by that name. JeeKao, the designated name used by one's contemporaries, came to welcome us. He was the postmaster general of Chengdu. He took his father, BeiFu, and his family to live with him. Then we went with Nan *laoscee* to a section of Saocheng, where only the Manchu people lived during the Ching dynasty. After the revolution of Sun Yat-sen, the Han people gradually began to move into this area too. Our landlord was a Manchurian, a "Chi-ren" or "flag person." These are relatives of the Emperor, and depending on the distance from His Highness, each family was designated a color. For instance, the Emperor's flag color was golden yellow, symbolized by the dragon; the red flag with the lion belonged to the Queen Mother; the blue flag with a weapon belonged to the paternal uncle; then white, another weapon, belonged to the maternal uncle; the other colors were sub-yellow, sub-red, sub-blue, and finally black, which was the Hsueh's flag. We were not related to the royal household, but we were the protectors, appointed by the Emperor, of the realm.

Our landlord called Srr (stone), though a typical Manchurian, was of a modern family. The eldest daughter studied wireless; the eldest son, SceYing, was studying in Chengdu; the second son was in Saocheng Secondary School. SceYing was curious about me because I was from the border area, so he was half sympathetic and half looked down on me. I only respected him because he was five years older than me. He even took me to his room in the back of the house to watch him do his calligraphy. He was considered to be a very good student, standing among the top ten in his class during examinations. Baba and his father often talked together at length, but Baba was worried that I, who tended to speak my mind, might say or do something inappropriate. He said to me, "ErTse, with people you do not know well, do not become too close or avoid them too much, or they may become suspicious of you."

When Baba and Mr. Srr spoke, I was surprised to hear Mr. Srr often used archaic words as if he wanted to impress Baba that he too knew classical Chinese, but Baba never let on that he himself was a classics scholar.

Wu LaoScee in Seng Yin Middle School

When I was walking, from Tser Tung Street to the SaoCheng Park one day, I took a wrong turn and ended up in the San Yin Street Middle School. Here, I saw posted on the gate that they were open to admit new students for the new term. I immediately entered the school and heard children's loud voices in the playground. I sought out the registration office; there was a man with a very long mustache talking to a younger man, presumably a teacher. When the mustached man saw me, he turned to me and said, "Have you come to enroll in this school? Tell me your name and how old you are. Where did you come from?"

I replied, "I was born in Dawu, went to Lucheng Elementary School, and now I am in Chengdu."

"Hey, slow down. Where did you say you come from?" he asked, puzzled.

"Dawu, also called TaoFu," I repeated.

"Never mind. Dawu, TaoFu—where is that exactly?" He was really puzzled now.

"Sorry, I spoke too fast. Dawu is at the border of Sichuan and Tibet."

"Oh, you are from the Sichuan border, the 'out of the gate' area. That is why I could not recognize the name of where you came from. Who else do you have at home?"

I told him the circumstances of my family and told him that our family was the border protectors of the emperor and that my name, Chi, was given to my family by Hsieng Fen Huang Di. I was tired of being looked down upon just because we were from the border area, "out of the gate," as he said. *Poof.*

"Oh," he said slowly, "so you are family related to the emperor [i.e., official]. Go bring a bench, sit, and we will talk awhile.

"My name is Wu. I am the principal of this school, which I built. I named this school Seng Ying, which means 'very good, very pure.' Our family was from Manchuria, the Seng Ying Ru Yang Camps, and our flag was pale yellow. You need not tell your family. It is the Han army—a great worker for the country. All these are in the past now. It is history. It is not worth remembering and to have any self-pity. Just do not forget one's roots. You study well and do something for *ren-ming*, the peasants." He paused for a while, shook his head in deep thought, then added, "Yes, we do need new students to be accepted. One must pass the entrance examination, but you need not. You seem qualified already. Tomorrow you may come and attend the school opening ceremony and start your schooling." Then he slowly walked away, stroking his long mustache, deep in thought, and shaking his head slowly from side to side.

I was extremely happy and told Mma and Baba what I had done when I returned home. Baba was proud of me and said, "Ha-ha-ha, how easily you have enrolled yourself into school."

PART II

HONG CHENG:
A TURBULENT LIFE

Chapter 1

OPENING CEREMONY OF SCHOOL

Early next morning, I joined the school's opening ceremony. At the entrance to the gate of the school, there was an engraved tablet dedicated to Kung FuTse (Confucius). The gate opened onto a wide path, which divided the school into two sections. On the left was the primary school section. There were two large classrooms facing each other, each of which could seat one hundred students. On the right side was the middle school, where a new building had just opened. Here, the basketball and volleyball courts and general playgrounds were situated. Between the two sections were the students' common room and the large assembly hall. It was here the opening ceremony was conducted. The principal, Wu LaoScee, and the teachers, dressed in the Ching-dynasty style of long black gowns and short jackets, were waiting in front of Kung FuTse's tablet. A loud announcement was heard throughout the school. "Let the school opening ceremony begin."

The principal stepped up onto the dais at the end of the assembly hall.

"All students and teachers, come to your positions." The announcer was the young master I had met yesterday, called Mr. Hay, who was the head teacher at the primary school section. Then a third announcement: "Foo."

I was baffled and did not know what that meant. I sneaked a glance around and saw all the teachers and students had knelt.

"Hsing." Everyone started to kowtow. After three of these, again, "Hsing." Everyone rose. "Foo." We all knelt again and kowtowed three times.

We repeated this three times, and I realized that this was the ancient way of school opening ceremonies. The principal then proclaimed the school was officially opened. He admonished us to study hard, be good, and obey our masters. Finally, an old teacher led us to our respective classrooms, which still smelled of new paint. This teacher introduced himself as Tsao SaoRen or Tsao LaoScee (teacher).

"I am the program master, and I am in charge of all your livelihood and behavior. Today we are not having any classes, so you may tour the school grounds and acquaint yourselves with the school."

"Master Tsao, does our school always follow the ancient customs of bowing and kowtowing every spring and autumn?" I asked respectfully.

Tsao LaoScee smiled and said, "No, no, only on Kung FuTse's birthday."

"Oh, we followed such customs at home, but ever since I started school, we just bowed, never kowtowed," I said.

"Ah," said Tsao LaoScee, "you are the child from Ta ChiengLu."

"Yes."

"We only do this kowtowing on Kung FuTse's birthday because of the principal. There is another school called Yin Whang School where they still do this every day."

"Who is the principal of that school?" I asked.

"Hsu TseLao. He is one of ChengDu's famous five old and seven scholars. Our own principal was a student of his. Go look around the school, get to know it, and then you may go home. We will talk again when we have another chance."

I walked to the middle school section on the right side of the dividing path to a small classroom, which sat twenty to thirty students. At the end of the classroom, I saw what seemed to be the living quarters of someone. I walked up to it and looked into the rectangular window, which had no glass but closed with the typical thin slightly opaque paper. On this was written a few poems, which I still remember:

During spring, I lay fast asleep,

Did not feel it was daybreak.

I heard birds singing everywhere

Around the air.

Last night, wind and raindrops

I know not how many flowers lay

Damaged on the ground.

The calligraphy was beautiful, and as I walked past the window, I saw a lovely garden with a pond full of lotus blossoms. Surrounding the pond were small palm trees, and behind these, a wall was hidden. Three steps from this enchanting garden was another classroom and, strangely enough, a small *shen-kan* (shrine) on either side of which were two doors, through which was yet another garden also grown with palms. In the middle of this garden was a well, and here, I saw Mr. Hay drawing water from the well.

"Master Hay," I called.

"Eh, you are the student who was talking with Tsao LaoScee. Come, sit here."

When asked, he told me that, indeed, the room with the papered windowpane was his. He put down his bucket carefully so as not to spill the water on the floor of his very tidy and clean room. I told him that Tsao LaoScee had told us to look around the school and get acquainted with the grounds and classrooms.

"Normally, the principal does not allow the younger students to wander about in case they mess up the school," he said.

"At the shen-kan, which god do you worship?" I asked.

"That is not a shen-kan. That is the Liu Juin's [the six scholars'] honored seat."

(It is considered all right to honor or "worship" renowned scholars, called Liu Juin Tse Shen-kan, among educated Chinese.)

"Please tell me about these Liu Juin Tse, if you have the time," I asked.

"Since we do not have classes today, I do have time," Mr. Hay answered.

"There must be an interesting story attached to this," I replied. "I am very interested in these sorts of stories. In which dynasty did they live? And what are their names?" I asked earnestly and eagerly.

Hay LaoScee said, "This is not ancient history. It happened during Kwang Hsue HwangDi's time during the Ching dynasty. During that time, there was a man called Khan YuWei and his student, Liang ChicChao. That wise man saw that the political situation was not good, so he had written many articles to encourage the change of some of the laws of the land, but no one paid any attention to him. Once he had written what he thought a fair treatise of the situation in the countryside, he decided to send it to the emperor. The emperor's tutor, Wu TangHo, read the article and realized that the author was an unusual and gifted person, so he called Khan Yu Wei to court and presented him to the emperor. The emperor read the paper and agreed with Khan YuWei's criticisms and tried to implement the advice therein. Unfortunately, the majority of the 'old guard' and eunuchs used the Empress Dowager's name and threw Khan YuWei out of court and banished him out of Peiping [now Beijing]. They also accused the emperor's own supporters as being anarchistic and disloyal to the country and destroyed them. Khan YuWei managed to escape with his life to Hong Kong then later to Japan." Then Hay LaoScee, pointing to the other five Juin Tse, said, "This is Wu Su TsenBing of the 1834 political upheaval, these other two are Oh TongHo, Tan TseTung, and Lian QinChao. I have forgotten the sixth Juin Tse. Since our principal was also a member of the royal pale-yellow flag family, he respected and honored the Liu JuinTse. Now you know why we have their shen-kan."

Then Hay LaoScee said that he had to go out. I wandered about the school grounds a bit more then returned home.

I found Mma was cleaning my white school uniform. During the summer school sessions, all students must wear white. This was a first time I had worn anything white other than for funeral rites.

Ta Chen Chung Middle School

There were three famous Middle Schools in ChengDu: (1) Union Middle, (2) ChengDu Middle, and (3) Hwa Yang Middle. These three schools had not only many students but also some of the best teachers, e.g., the famous English teacher, Kung HsiangLung; the mathematics teachers, Wang BeiNee and Ko JiYung; and Tsao SaoHan, the work analyst teacher. All the schools fought for these teachers. Though our school was the newest, our principal had been student of Wu Lou Tse Shing, one of the famous five scholars, so he was able to get two of the four. The principal himself taught work analysis. The principal of Ta Cheng Chung Middle school was Hsue TseChing, our principal's son, so the two schools became "brother schools." Hsue TseChing taught botany.

We were taken to visit that middle school and felt that our school was not up to par because our school was small, and we were a combination of primary and middle schools. Our gym equipment and playground were far inferior, but we envied them their football field most of all.

When Hsu TseLao hsiensen had started Ta Cheng Middle School, he had hoped to combine ancient and modern Chinese culture under one institution. He was considered to be one of the five scholars and seven famous persons and should have been successful. He was a scholar and was not very good at doing practical things, so he asked his friend Fung Lao, a man of tremendous presence—like the sound of a waterfall, as Hsu TseLao used to call him—to help him. Alas, this man died before the project was finished and long before I was able to meet him. His friend Hsu TseLao wrote this couplet for him:

Out of Five Elders, only two were left, Now you too are gone and left me alone, When you reach the Nether River and meet our three friends, Please convey to them, I shall be joining you all soon.

Chapter 2

MEETING OF OLD FRIENDS

I was surprised to receive a letter from Hwa ChungJuin from Nanking. We had said good-bye in LuCheng (Khanding) when he left for Peiping (Beijing). From there, he went to Nanjing and was there for two years. After a year, he thought he may return to LuCheng but had not yet decided. He had hoped that we could meet in Nanjing and talk about that, but by coincidence, he was already in Chengdu. All my childhood friends from LuCheng—Wang MungChow, Wang SheiFung, Chang Yi, and another primary schoolmate—all came to Chengdu; MungChow and ChungJuin had come from Sen Yang through Nanking back to Chengdu. "Old City" met "New City" friends—the happiness we all felt at seeing one another was indescribable. During those days of political turmoil, when we parted, we had not known if we would ever meet again.

MungChow also brought up the fact that another of our schoolmates and our principal of our primary school in LuCheng was in ChangAnn and suggested we invite him to come and meet with all of us in Chengdu. We sent him a telegram addressed to "Teacher Chang," primary school, Khanding. Ah, the optimism of youth. After three days, we received a letter from Principal Chang, saying that he and his students would come in the afternoon of the fourth day. After school the next day, I went to MungChow's hotel to arrange to go to the dock to receive Teacher Chang. On the way, I saw an elderly man in a long blue gown wearing a pair of soft-soled shoes. He was carrying a bundle over his right shoulder, and in his left hand, he played with three brass balls. I knew at once that he was Chang LaoScee. I called out to MungChow and the other friends, "Hey, you all, Chang Lao-scee is here."

They all came out of the hotel and ran to greet him. Teacher Chang stroked his beard and looked at us, from one to the other and back again. A large grin spread across his face. Then looking at me, he said, "You have grown so tall. You may be the youngest, but you are the tallest."

"Of course, I am almost graduated from middle school," I retorted.

"Ah, time has passed so quickly."

MungChow then asked, "Did our Yu schoolmate not come?"

"Yes, he is here. I left him at the river. Perhaps he got caught in the crowd." I remembered with what difficulty we had to cross the river when we traveled from Lucheng to Chengdu. Then we saw Yu come panting up the hill and, seeing Teacher Chang cried, "How did you get here so fast? I did not see you get off the ferry or on the bus. How did you get here so fast?" He looked annoyed.

"Aya, never mind," Chang LaoScee said. "The main thing is we are all together now." He looked around and said, "You are no longer so short and fat, MungChow," and to me, "You have grown so tall." He could not get over that.

"Come, come," said MungChow, "come inside the hotel, and we will talk. We should not block the street."

I took Chang LaoScee's bundle and discovered that there was no bedding or luggage but only a sword and musical instrument. I suspected that he was not human but one of those characters out of the ancient storybooks—people who could travel here and there without sleep or food. He looked upright and had an unusually relaxed expression on his face. I was extremely curious and spoke up. "Chang LaoScee, can you please teach me how to swordplay?"

The others looked at me as if I were mad, but Teacher Chang smiled and replied, "So you noticed that I have a sword and a *ching* [a seven-stringed instrument] in my bag. My mother gave this *ching* to me, and the sword has been handed down to me through four generations. It is over three hundred years old, and I carry them around with me everywhere I go, one for the love of my mother and, the second, in memory of my ancestors. Alas, I can neither play the *ching* nor can I swordplay. My family came from Malaysia in Southeast Asia, and we were lead miners. I came all the way to SiKhang to start another lead mining business, but I had no idea how to run a business, and soon I lost all my money and became bankrupt. I even considered suicide because I had let my family down. I have now come here to tell you a bit of my background. I must leave tomorrow for Ching Cheng San." But he never did have the time to tell us his story, and till this day, I have no idea what kind of a man he was or where he went.

Then he turned to Yu. "Yu Tungsho, you go back to YaChow first. We are all Buddhists [*yuan fa*], and our friendship is predestined. Let us all be happy. Let us drink to our health, drink wine—or tea, if you do not drink wine."

As he spoke, I never took my eyes off those three metal balls he was playing with all the time—rolling them in the palm of his right hand, running them up his arm and down again, twirling them around his wrist—as if they were tethered to his fingers.

I was most amazed, but as soon as he noticed my concentrated curiosity, he let them roll back into his palm quietly. This was one of the happiest moments of my days since I took my brush and started my remembrances. Such happiness cannot be repeated with Chang *LaoScee* because if he were alive today, he would be one hundred and twenty-five years old.

MungChow Takes Up a Job in ChengDu

Chang Yi, Wang SheiFun, Hwa ChungJuin, and the other two friends left ChengDu to return to Khanding. MungChow decided to stay and found a job in Chengdu, so he moved from the hotel to stay in his maternal uncle's house. We, on the other hand, had to move again. We were living on the Ching Hwa Bridge side, but soon, the place was too small for us because my uncle and his concubine and baby cousin sister also came to live with us. Baba was fond of his brother, so he allowed his family to live with us. We moved into a place in Persimmon Lane, which was a much larger single-family building and could accommodate everyone. As soon as we moved, my cousin—my third uncle's son, the postmaster general of SceeJian—was transferred to Chengdu to be the head postmaster here. He lived with his father-in-law who was the director of transportation of the Twenty-eighth Army. He had introduced Uncle to the Mung Kung District to work at the section of planning and development, i.e., to develop barren land. However, shortly thereafter, Uncle returned because he became seriously ill. He had been diagnosed with dysentery, for which Baba gave him some herbal medicines, but this had no effect, so a professional Chinese doctor was called. This doctor gave Uncle three doses of medicine, but after the third one, there was still no improvement. The old doctor took Uncle's pulse and got angry. He threw down his wrist and said, "This patient does not look after himself; he drinks and visits the pleasure houses too much. I have no further prescriptions for him"; but the old doctor calmed down, prescribed more medicine, then angrily left. Later, Uncle's illness worsened, but every time he got out of bed to go the bathroom, he only wanted me to help and hold on to because he did not feel safe with anyone else. Then he told Baba and his son, "See that young Number Four? He is our Hsueh family's real latter generation. To look at him, he seems so soft and gentle, but his hands and arms are strong. To hold him is like holding an iron rod. We all descended from warriors and generals, but except for him, we have all become soft scholars." Then looking down at me, he continued, "Only you can follow the times, and never let it defeat you." These were his last words. His head fell on my shoulders, and his grip on my arm went limp.

My cousin cried, "Father, you cannot leave. You cannot throw us all away without care."

Baba fell on the floor and cried, "Elder Brother, come back. Come back."

Small Auntie was so overwrought that she repeatedly banged her head on the wall, and we were afraid she would do serious damage to herself. Mma held her back and held little cousin sister who was screaming and yelling. I took Uncle and put him on the bed and closed his eyes and mouth. Then we chanted, "BeiFu, go quietly. We will take care of everything and will return all that is yours." Baba then took care of the burial rites—simple and sad. Then he told cousin brother that he was being sent to Yueh Shi District to be the district secretary. This new job was about a ten-day horseback ride from Chengdu and was not ideal, and he did not want to take his now-much-extended family with him. So he asked Cousin Brother to look for a smaller less expensive place for all of us to live before he left. Cousin Brother GeeKow said to Baba, "As it happens, Vice Postmaster General Liu YaoChing is building a new mansion, and I think he will rent it to you at a discount. The rooms are big and airy, and there is a small vegetable garden in the back. It is a bit far from the market and close to the army training field of Chengdu, but it will be quiet and peaceful, quite good for a family." Baba decided to take it.

"Third Uncle, if you must leave immediately, Third Aunt, Younger Sister, and Fourth brother [me] can come and live with us till Liu YaoChing's house is ready."

So our family moved again from Jung Hwa Bridge, *Xiao Chen* (or Small Town), a Manchurian section, to the Western Gate section. Liu YaoChing's house was called Yao Pu, which consisted of two buildings adjacent to each other, and behind this was a large vegetable garden. At the front and near the buildings was a row of shops. This was indeed a reasonably priced and well-constructed brick house. We moved in. All the post office workers called the vice postmaster general Iron Abacus because of his miserliness, but he did not spare expenses on this house.

Parting of Father and Son

Before the move had finished, Baba had already started preparing for his journey. One morning, I saw the new worker quickly make ready Baba's luggage and instinctively knew that he was going to follow him to Yueh Shu. Baba was already dressed and had a black armband around his left arm inscribed with the name of the deceased, my second uncle; and then facing Uncle's tablet and bowing, I heard him praying softly, "Brother, Elder Brother, your spirit is not far. I beg you to look after my family." Then with tears in his eyes, he turned toward to Mma. "I am going away now. I have tried my best to take care of you and our family, but times are changing, and I do not know how long I will be away this time. You must take care of yourself now."

My mother used to indulge herself occasionally by smoking opium when my father was away on one of his longer trips, but since that day, I never saw her take up her pipe again. The little maidservant confided in me that she had broken it even before Baba was out of sight.

I followed Baba's carriage out of the Western Gate and continued to follow him on foot for more than a mile. Then Baba ordered the carriage to stop and got out and walked toward me. "Come, ChiPei, *ertse* [son], you should not go any further. Go, go, go home. Go back to your mother, and you must take good care of her. She is too much of a lady." I tried to kowtow to him, but he grabbed me and tried to lift me up and said, "This ground is too dirty. Don't kowtow." I was usually afraid of my father's stern face and never went against his words, but this time I disobeyed him and continued kneeling on the ground. Tears flowed down my cheeks, which I was afraid to show Baba, a sign of weakness he would have remonstrated. But Baba knelt too and took me in his arms, took out his handkerchief, and wiped away my tears. Then he wiped away his own tears.

"Do not cry," he said. "Don't be sad. Times will get better."

I had never felt my Baba so kind and so close. In my young and optimistic mind, I never imagined that this would be the last time we would see each other. I thought that because of our sudden misfortune and the death of Uncle, he had to leave and get a job somewhere else. Suddenly, he looked up to the sky and shouted, "Oh, heaven, why are you so cruel to us?"

My head was still bowed to the ground, and when I looked up from my kowtowing position, his carriage was already in the distant horizon.

"Farewell, Baba, farewell." I never saw him again. He died of dysentery a few years later. He was not yet sixty.

Move to YaoPu

We rose early next morning after Baba's departure to pack and prepare for our move to our new abode. Mma was taken to PaoTai, Uncle's wife, to avoid the confusion while we started to move things over. By four in the afternoon, we were done. The house was a short distance between Xiao Cheng and the Northern Army Training Field. One of Baba's colleagues, Mr. Yao, from the Ming An District, also moved close to us as our neighbor. The rooms in the house were arranged in a square around a large "living cum shrine" room. On one side was my third sister and Mma's room; on the other was my cousin brother and his wife's room. My little room was upstairs. Behind the shrine was the kitchen and bathroom. Later, my friend MungChow came to share my room. He paid my cousin twenty yuan a month for his room and board. Baba sent Mma one hundred yuan a month, out of which sixty was given to cousin brother, for our expenses. I was not clear as to what all this meant, but I learned that the normal cost of living in those days per month for a family like ours was but five yuan a month! It turned out that, on the grounds that he was a colleague of Baba's, Mr. Yao did not want to pay his share. He grumbled and quarreled with my cousin, who eventually asked him to leave. So now Mungchow and I moved down into Mr. Yao's much larger room, and my little room became a guest room.

Almost every night MungChow (MC in future) and I used to play our music in our room, and Cousin GeeKow would hear us when he returned from his nightly mahjong games. One night, he looked in on us and asked if he could join us as he knew how to play the bamboo flute. We then formed the Three Yellow Music Club. GooKao played the flute, MC the lute, and I the harmonium—or the flute also when GooKao was too busy. We were very proud of our music club and our music, and often neighbors would come and listen to us.

One day GeeKow received an obituary notice, saying that his mother-in-law had died. He had to go to his father's house to help with the family affairs so that he could neither play mahjong nor join in our musical evenings. He did this for five weeks as was the custom and, at the end of the fifth week, had to go for the entire night to take care of the final funeral rites. He returned extremely late the following night. He called me, saying, "Fourth Brother, I am exhausted, so tonight we will not play music. Please tell MC."

"It is 9:00 p.m. and late. I am going to bed too. I will put the bedside candle closer to me and read instead." At about 10:00 p.m., I heard sister-in-law cry out, "GeeKow, GeeKow, GeeKow," but cousin never answered. He was sound asleep.

"Your cousin can really sleep. After only fifteen minutes, he is so soundly asleep. Even such crying cannot wake him," whispered MC and laughing softly, but he had barely finished speaking when we heard Auntie scream and scream.

"Aya, Fourth Brother, come and see what has happened to your big brother." I jumped out of bed, knocking down the bedside candle in the process.

"You stupid clumsy boy, you'll burn the house down next," scolded MC.

I rushed to cousin brother's room and found Auntie pinching Brother's philtrum (which is the way Chinese doctors revive a person who had fainted). I felt his forehead, which was cold with sweat.

"I will call Dr. Chung of Bei Tsai Hospital," and ran to the hospital to fetch him. Fortunately, Dr. Chung was there. He immediately grabbed his bag and jumped into his carriage. We got home as quickly as possible; but when we arrived, Mma, Auntie, and Small Auntie were throwing rice about my cousin. This meant that he had already died, and they were trying to ward off evil spirits. We waited until the end of ritual before Dr. Chung felt cousin's pulse. He frowned, then listened to his heart, pounded his chest, and, at last, announced sadly, "He cannot be saved." Upon hearing this, Sister-in-law fell on her knees in front of the doctor and begged him to bring her husband back to life. Meanwhile, Sister-in-law's adopted daughter and her husband, who had just returned from the USA, came in. When they saw what was going on and saw her adoptive father on the deathbed, she rushed out of the house without shoes on her tiny bound feet. Later, she told me that she had felt as if she only had a pair of stubs, no feet.

"Dr. Chung, save his life. Please save his life."

"There is no pulse, no breath, no hope. What can I do? Aya!"

The son-in-law from America asked, "What sort of illness did he die of?"

"Heart failure." We had never heard of this kind of illness; even the American PhD was stunned.

"I do not usually go out in the middle of the night. But because you, ChiPei, came to fetch me personally, I came. I am sorry, but there is nothing I can do. Please quickly prepare for his burial."

I told number two servant to take the doctor home, then turned, and saw the entire family crying like one huge bucket of tears. Sister-in-law, who had walked here only in her socks, had fainted; even the two servant girls were tearlessly wailing. Sister-in-law's American Chinese husband marveled that how the dead man's wife could have walked on her "operated foot" on such stony ground for such a long way. It was pitiful. Wang Sao, the maidservant, tried to put another pair of shoes on her without avail. I touched Sister-in-law gently on her shoulders, and she immediately sat up and once again started to wail, "GeeKow, GeeKow, get up, get up. I will go with you." Her voice was so tragic, and we all burst out crying once more.

Finally, I said, "Big Sister-in-law, we cannot allow Big Brother to go like this. We must buy a coffin, paint it, and buy death clothes, hat, sock, and shoes. Get a priest to pray for us, rent a tent, prepare the burial table, and so many things to do. We must prepare all this."

At last, Sister-in-law realized the amount of work to be done and said, "Yes, yes, I have a brother who is a major in the army. He may be able to come in an hour or two and help us. Second Brother is not in Chengdu. Third Brother is under training and cannot take leave. That leaves the eldest brother, Tse TaYeh, but he is useless. He can only play mahjong. Finally, I have Fourth Brother who is four years older than you, ChiPei, but this young man is not only useless but a small-time crook." Then she turned to MC and kowtowed to him. "Brother, you and our fourth brother are like blood brothers, but ChiPei is still too young, so you must help him."

MC picked her up and said, "Please, do not worry. I will assist in everything."

"First we must get a *feng shui* specialist for the burial site," said Sister-in-law. "Sister-in-law," announced MC, "the *feng shui* specialist is right here," and he pointed to himself.

"Oh," said PhD from America. Sister-in-law did not understand. "Oh," said PhD, again, "You are an educated modern person, and yet you still believe in such things?" he added, very surprised and amused.

MC replied, "If you were to ask me to find a plot of land where the latter generation will flourish and become rich, I cannot find. But if you were to ask me to find a plot of land for burial, a dry place for the body, and a place easy for relatives to come and pay respect, this I can find."

Early next morning I went to Jing Hwa Bridge see an artist named Chen BeiLing to ask him to paint a portrait of my cousin to put on his spiritual tablet. When I told Mr. Chen that my older cousin had died, he jumped up and exclaimed, "Aya, Aya, why is it that your household has lately been plagued by so many misfortunes? First, your uncle died. Then you father got transferred far away, and now your older cousin is dead. I had wanted him to help me clear up a family debt owed to us. Now all that is finished. Even there is no opportunity to talk. How come he died so suddenly? He was so young and generous. How was this possible? Did you say the Hsueh family had three sons? You had not mentioned anything about your oldest uncle. Now your second uncle is dead, and your own father is so far away on work. What will happen to you and your family? You are too young, even younger than me, to have such heavy burdens on your young shoulders."

He rattled on. He was talking about me, but actually, he was talking about himself too. His family was also a flag family that had fallen into hard times. Then he repeated, "First Elder Uncle whom you did not know, then Second Elder Uncle died, and now even your older cousin brother has passed away. Your family ... and your father so far away. Now you must bear this heavy burden on your young shoulders. You are younger than me. Your life is so bitter"—and shaking his head— "so pitiful." As he spoke, tears ran down his face. His forebears had started to serve in the palace in 'Peiping' during the Chin dynasty, during the reign of the Sixth Emperor Hsieh Fung, about a thousand years ago. Gradually, as times and politics changed, some of the flag people moved from 'Peiping' to Sichuan. Most of these people lived in Xiao Cheng near Ching Hwa Bridge. His own family had done the move at the end of the nineteenth century. Mr. Cheng Beilin's parents, his three brothers, and sister had always lived beside Ching Hwa Bridge. He had only finished primary schooling and was doing odd jobs here and there, and any earnings he made, he handed over to his father. Later, his father took him to the Christian Church School where he joined the Bible class and learned English. Soon, the teachers discovered that his handwriting was beautiful, and he was encouraged to draw and paint. His fourteen-year-old sister was sent to a family to be a servant girl, who later became a concubine of the master, the headmaster of the Sichuan Technical College. All instructions were taught in English, and at that time, everything was handwritten because there were no typewriters. Beilin became the chief scribe and earned about twenty yuans a month with which he supported his family. He and I considered ourselves "hard times" friends.

"Please, Beilin, I need you to paint a portrait of my cousin brother to put it on his spiritual tablet. I need it by tomorrow as his death was so sudden."

"Did you bring a photo of your cousin?"

"Yes, only of his face."

He laughed and said, "That's all I need." Then he asked me for fifty fens. I gave him five silver yuans. He said, amazed, "I only need fifty fens to buy a piece of cardboard. I do not need anything else. Today I am not busy. I do not have any classes until Friday afternoon, and I have already prepared my lectures, so I will be able to paint Elder Cousin's portrait by this afternoon. Meet you later at Yao Pu's."

Then I went to the coffin maker, who saw me and said, "Do not worry. Mr. Wong has already been here, and we have sent everything over. Even the painter has gone with the sealer. We need to apply seven layers of paint, one layer a day to allow for drying time. Therefore, we need seven days."

When I returned home, I saw that Elder Cousin's paper garments were already on. He looked grand in his scholar's long dark-blue gown, light-blue long-sleeved undershirt whose cuffs and collars could just be seen poking out from under the robe, white socks on his feet, and a pair of black shoes outside. His head was crowned with a black-and-organza scholars' hat and his long whiskers neatly combed in front of his gown. Elder Cousin Sister-in-law was lying on the floor, quietly weeping, and another cousin was also crying. Seeing me, he wiped his nose, clicked his heels, and bowed to me because he was in uniform. I called, "Chieng Big Brother." He replied, "Fourth Brother." We looked at each other with tear-filled eyes. Without another word, I finally realized the full meaning of the words of the Sun Tsao poet:

"Tear-filled eyes face tear-filled eyes."

He sighed and, catching his breath, said, "Fourth Brother, my sister's … death rites … you alone bearing responsibilities. We cannot thank you enough."

"Chieng Brother, we are close relatives, no formalities please. Whether I can or cannot shoulder the responsibilities, I must do so. Please instruct me."

"If GeeKow Brother knew, he too will be grateful to you." Chieng Brother then held me with both hands, tears coursing down his face but could not utter a single word. I knew he was extremely fond of his brother-in-law.

The coffin bearers arrived to prepare the body for burial. They had bought a big round of thick bread to put into the coffin. I asked them, "Why are you putting that bread into the coffin?"

"In case the dead is not dead—this has happened before—then there will be something for him to eat. But the real reason is to keep the rats from gnawing on the body if they should get in."

"What a terrible thought," I shuddered.

"What time is the actual ceremony?"

"Noon. There are only three more minutes."

"But where are the monks and others?" I asked, slightly annoying the bearers at my impatience and nosiness. At that very moment, they all arrived plus the two bearers of musical instruments. Cheng Beilin also arrived, carrying the portrait of my cousin. I saw that it was a very close likeness of him, and everyone exclaimed when he or she saw it and declared that they did not know that Cheng Beilin was such a good artist.

"What else can I do? I am useless otherwise," he said.

"Everything is ready except that the people who are supposed to raise the marquis have not yet arrived."

"Then I will go and tell them to hurry up," said Beilin.

I persuaded Elder Cousin Sister-in-law, who was still kneeling in front of her dead husband, to sit on a chair, which she flatly refused. Finally, her brother said, "DaJieh [Elder Sister], please, if you continue to kneel by the coffin, they cannot perform the death rites. Also, Fourth Cousin Brother needs your help. Last night, he ran hither and thither arranging this and that without stopping his hands and feet. If he becomes exhausted, what can we do then?" Elder Cousin Sister-in-law allowed herself to be escorted to a chair and sat down. The coffin bearers, Sau MingSeu and his elder brother, put Cousin Brother into the coffin and called loudly, "Close the coffin," whereupon Cousin Sister-in-law rushed to the coffin and held on to the lid it was impossible for the bearers to close it and nail down the lid. Once more, her brother and I pulled her away, and the coffin was finally shut.

The monks started to beat their drums, play their flutes, and pray *Tsow du ching* (rites of passage into death). Cousin Sister-in-law fainted, so I told Wang Sao to put a quilt on the floor, and with Chieng DaGe's help (big brother), we gently put her on it and softly tried to comfort her. I asked the PhD husband of the adopted daughter to go and fetch his wife, Hung Kuang, to come and take care of her adoptive mother. She came and immediately rushed to her mother's side. "Kan-ma, kan-ma [adoptive mother]." Hung Kuan was a childhood friend of mine. Had she not called out "kan-ma," I would not have recognized this young woman. Cousin Sister-in-law took her into her arms and cried out aloud, and they rocked and cried together, and so passed such a confused moment. The coffin was sealed, and all the monks had finished their prayers. It was the turn of the painters to start work. Everyone had arrived, the shrine was set, the marquis was erected, and the coffin was being painted. Mma and my Jiehjieh (elder sister) looked after the female guests while MC and I took care of the males. Cheng Beilin ran the errands outside.

The Burial Site

The week passed quickly. Elder Cousin Sister-in-law asked about the location of the burial site, so I discussed with MC and decided that we had to return to the area where my uncle was buried. That land belonged to the Kwei Chow People's Association, and we were from Kwei Chow, so it was fitting that we should use it. That area was called the Ten Lamb's Field and was about three to four li from Chengdu and was reached by going through the marketplace. Early next morning MC and I hired a wheelbarrow (a common mode of transportation, called a cock cart, which was invented by Chu Guo Kung Ming in AD 216) to take us to the graveyard.

The cock-cart driver said, "Will you be returning to town?"

"Yes," we answered.

"Then I will wait for you because this road passes by my house on the way to town."

Over the centuries, the wheels of the cock carts had formed a deep rut on the path, so it was fairly easy to travel to the graveyard; and by 11:00 a.m., we reached the field. First, we went to pay respect to my uncle's gravestone, which was still new and sharp. I bowed over his grave, and tears filled my eyes. MC also bowed respectfully, and turning to me, he said, "You must be strong and stand tall. Do not imitate all those women crying all the time. Don't go against your own character. Don't be like those women." I knew he was right, and I should not be so sentimental. I told the driver that we would be here for about one and a half hours. Then we will return to town.

"One hour will be enough. I will go home, then come back for you in one hour's time. My house is next to the manager of the field," he said.

Then MC and I started to find the grave plot. He taught me the principles of feng shui (wind and water) of burial sites: the land must be dry, the foreground must be open, and there should be a small hill or a forest in the back.

Since we did not have much time, we ran around hither and thither but could not find a suitable spot. I was hot and took off my hat to wipe my brow. Suddenly, I saw vaguely a man dressed in black in the distance, not too far from us on a small slope, as if he was looking for something. I turned to MC to tell him, and when I turned back, the man was gone. However, there, where the apparition had appeared, was indeed an empty plot with all the aspects that MC had described. I looked around

115

everywhere for that man but found no one. I remembered that before Elder Cousin Brother's coffin was secured, he was dressed in the same attire as the man. I softly prayed and thanked him for helping us.

"I hope, Elder Cousin Brother, this is the plot you wish to be buried in." Then I shouted to MC, "MungChow, MungChow, come quickly, quickly." MC rushed over and scolded me again, "Are you crazy? Why are you shouting and screaming? I thought that you had fallen down or stepped on a snake or something awful. What is the matter?" He was genuinely quite cross with me.

"I have found the gravesite," I replied.

"Where is it?"

"Here it is." Then I told him about the apparition, which he did not believe and scolded me again of having lost my reason.

"How can this be? If he had been a ghost, surely, he would not have appeared at midday, hmmmm?"

"Oh, all right, spirit or not, come and look at the site," I retorted.

Then he placed all his gravesite-locating instruments on it and looked up and said seriously, "Yes, this is it. Your Ta-Ge [big brother] has picked the perfect spot." We prepared this site for the formal burial, which would take place forty-two days hence. When all was decided and prepared, the cart driver returned with the graveyard manager, to whom we showed the plot we had picked, and he said that they would not dig until we were ready to bury the dead in case it rained. Then he looked at MC and called him reverent sir in spite of the latter's youth because he thought he was an expert gravesite diviner. I laughed and said, "He is only my third elder brother."

"Ah, Third Master," said the cock-cart driver, "you are clever to find such a good plot in one hour." He then sighed. "Life is not fair. Your second uncle was buried but a few weeks ago and now his son, who is barely thirty years old." He sighed again and continued, "Those who are fortunate cannot live long to enjoy their good fortune, but those who are unfortunate must continue to live and suffer. Look at me. I am fifty-two, and I still have to push this cock cart. During the rainy season, the ruts are so bad that it takes me two days to get to town and back when it normally takes only one day. I get paid for one day, Aya." He sighed yet again. "Life is full of injustices. It is intolerable, such harsh weather, and sometimes we must take abuses. People call me turtle and shout at me for crawling like a turtle." (*Turtle* is one of the worst things one can be called.)

"Why can't you also swear back at them?" I asked innocently.

"Aya, how can I say anything to those soldiers and businessmen?"

When we reached town, we gave him three pieces of silver. He was so taken aback that he refused to take them, saying, "It is too much. I cannot accept so much."

"Just consider this as a gift, old sir," I said, "from me to your family. Have a feast on us."

"Ah, all right, all right, this I will do. My family can eat pork tonight. If you ever come this way again, you must come to my house for an ordinary country folk's meal. We may not be rich, but we have our own chickens. Along my house is a stream where we can catch fresh fish. I am sure you people have never eaten such fresh things."

"Okay, if we take your cart when we return to this field, then we certainly will go to your house. But if you are busy that day, we will go to visit you anyway. Let us be friends." The old man grinned from ear to ear, muttering all the while, "Don't mention it. Don't mention it."

When MC and I went to the Ten-Sheep Field a second time to inter my Da-Ge, we were unable to visit the old man; we, never saw him again. I hope he and his family have experienced the peace and contentment and appreciated his good fortune of having a family, raised chickens, and freshly caught fish in a nearby stream.

On the fifth week after Ta-Ge's death, at four o'clock in the afternoon, we all were just sitting down to our evening meal when a village woman carrying a small child came into the house and went straight to Ta-Ge's spiritual tablet. She fell before it and started to cry.

"Ge-ge [Big Brother], how can you be gone?" Mma went to pull her away and realized that she was Jin Kuan ta-jieh (Elder Sister). She had only just received my letter written two weeks ago, telling her of Ta-Ge's passing. They could not come to the funeral because, being farmers, they were in the middle of harvesting. When Cousin Sister-in-law saw Jing ta-jieh, she began to cry again so that even Mma, Third Sister, and our maid started to weep too. Jun Kuan and Ta-Ge had grown up together and had been extremely close, almost like father and daughter. Mma held ta-jieh and told everyone to stop crying. "If we cry any more, we will frighten this little one. What is the name of your baby?" asked Mma, trying to distract everyone. Jing Kuan recovered a bit and answered, "My daughter is called Hwei-Chung" and told the child to call Mma Third Grandmother.

Gradually, everyone calmed down, and the crying abated. Jing Kuan ta-jieh stayed with us for a few days. Then she returned to their farm amid many tears and moans and groans as we all said good-bye. I never saw her again.

Dynamics of Family and Friend Relationships

Before my third uncle died, he had arranged with the postmaster general to deposit 2,500 silver yuan for his son and daughter-in-law, my *Ta-Sao*, Elder-Cousin Sister. Now that Big Cousin Brother was dead and had been buried barely a week, the postmaster general's secretary, plus four of his colleagues, came to pay a visit to Elder Cousin Sister-in-law, Ta-Sao. MC and I were just discussing as to how to pacify the family when we suddenly heard *Ta-Sao* cry out, "I kneel before you all. I never knew Ta-Ge owed you any money, and now you want me to repay you. From where can I get this money?"

"Ta-Sao," the men said, "this is not the way to speak. You have 2,500 silver yuan from GeeKow's postmaster's pension. We are only asking you for nine hundred of the silver, which he owed us. Please pay us now!" he demanded.

MC heard this and suddenly stood up and shouted with authority, "And how did you know about Ta-Sao's 2,500 silver yuan pension? This money was deposited and saved in your post office for Hsueh Ta-Sao as assistance to widow and the orphan. If Hsueh GeeKow did actually owe you money, then there must be some written record. Let me see it." MC demanded, "Then we will find a solution to this so-called debt."

"What is your name? Who are you? This debt is between GeeKow and us. What is it to you, eh?"

MC replied indignantly, "I am an old schoolmate of Fourth Brother here. We were in LuCheng together, and I am an old family friend. I have been living with the Hsueh family ever since I returned from the northeast. I pay them twenty yuans a month for my room and board, so I know Hsueh GeeKow was taking care of all the family accounts. He was a very organized and meticulous man and wrote everything down. If he owed you anything, I am sure he will have a record of it. Go fetch this evidence." MC finished sternly.

"This money was hard earned by us," whined the men.

"Aside from thievery, robbery, cheating, lying, or gambling, what kind of money is not earned, eh?" asked MC.

Then they turned to my Ta-Sao again, "Please, Ta-sao, have pity on us and return us our money."

Before Ta-Sao could reply, I quickly said, "If you want to talk about pity, it is Ta-Sao who is pitiful. If you don't have any money today, you could go to work tomorrow and earn money. All my Ta-Sao had was Ta-Ge, and now he is dead. What can she do? She depends on that pension for the rest of her life! You are supposed to be Ta-Ge's friends, and you should have offered her some help. Instead, you have come to make claims for which you have no proof. If your claim is correct, let me know the amount, and I will pay you for Hsueh GeeKow."

They looked amazed and happily asked me, "Do you really mean it?"

"Of course," I replied, "only if what you say is true, but I will need time to get it."

"How long?"

"When I graduate from university, I will pay you 10 percent monthly, *but* you must give me an exact amount and show me the record!"

"Fourth Brother, how can we? Hsueh GeeKow lost his money

gambling." Now MC piped up, "Eh! So? This is gambling money? Debts incurred on the gambling table should be paid and settled at the gambling table. This is a misfortune for the GeeKow's family, but it is your bad luck that GeeKow is dead because, at the gambling table, who owed whom, who should pay whom, and how much, who knows, eh, eh? Those debts should all be settled at that time. You have *no* right to claim this debt, so be off and forget this episode." MC grinned with satisfaction.

The men ignored MC, nodded to Ta-Sao, said, "See you later," and left.

Ta-Sao turned to MC and said, "Aya, Mung Chow, will they really return?"

"No, they will not now. They know they have no case, but don't be afraid. Even if they do, we can deal with them. It is unthinkable that people of such position can behave like this."

Baba wrote to say that he had heard about a Ta-Ge's death, and Ta-Sao's pension had already been sent to Ta-Sao's father because she had already made up her mind to move back to her parents' home. The next day she started to get ready, so the servants began to pack everything only in her room. She did not want anything else. Without her share of the rent, our home was too large and now too expensive for my mother and me, so we had to move again. I went to say good-bye to Ta-Sao.

"Is there anything you want?" she asked.

"I wanted only a thing as a memory of Ta-Ge, i.e., his fountain pen. He had told me that he would either give me his pen or buy me a new one when I go to Nanking University."

"Aya." She sighed. "You and your cousin were fond of each other. He often talked about giving his pen to you as soon as you went to university, but it is broken, and now he is gone."

"*Sao-Sao*, I know the pen is a broken and leaks. One cannot get parts for it in Chengdu, when I go to Nanking, I will take it with me, I am sure I can get repaired there. Every time I use it, I will think of Da-Ge." She gave me the pen, and I took it with great gladness and sadness. The rubber ink tube was indeed very old and leaky because the rubber had cracked with age, but it had a very good nib. When I replace it with a new one, I'm sure it will be as good as new. I had this pen all the time I was in Nanking, but during a simulated battle combat, I finally lost it. All my friends knew the history of my pen as being the only souvenir of my Ta-Ge, so they all helped me look for it. When the prefect heard about it, he gave us permission to search for it the entire day. Indeed, it was like looking for a "small fish in the ocean." We returned empty-handed and disappointed at the end of the day. I did not want my dinner and instead went to the classroom to write in my diary.

An old classmate, LaoLiu, from Ching Hai, came to tell me that when he had just passed the entrance examination for the Nanking University, his father suddenly died. He had not wanted to go to Nanking because he had not wanted to leave his old mother and younger brother at home alone, but they had forced him to do so. Last summer he had tried to return to Ching Hai to visit his mother and brother, but the trip would have been too long and expensive, so he did not go. I was puzzled as to why he should confide in me such things. Then I realized he had come to give me some advice about "letting go" of certain things.

"You must remember," he said, "that a man is often followed by bad fate, so you should not be so grave about things. To be a great man, one should be able to not only carry the burden but also know when to put it down."

I thanked him for his advice and told him that I had to finish the articles I was writing for the university magazine, which must be submitted before midnight to be published. I had also requested permission from the prefect to stay over at the classroom until 2:00 a.m. and to report to assembly at breakfast rather than the usual time of 6:00 a.m. for the morning exercises. Fifty years later, Lao Liu's word remained with me, but it is a variation of a common Chinese proverb: "Eight to nine times out of ten, things are not what they seem."

When the lights went off at 9:30 p.m., a cleaning boy came to my classroom with a *tiffin carrier* (boxed dinner). He had brought for me a dish of duck, noodles, and bean cake.

"Why did you spend so much money for this food?" I asked.

"I did not. Today is my grandma's birthday, so my father bought these dishes to celebrate. I simply brought little leftovers for you, knowing that you had to burn the candle till 2:00 a.m."

"I will eat the noodles, but please take the other things home. Thank you."

"No, I will leave the bean cake in case you get hungry later."

This boy was young but very clever, but because his family was poor, he had to leave school and get a job. We became friends, and I was sympathetic toward him. He was also very fond of me. Often, I used to teach him some Chinese history and literature. However, when I left Nanking, I wrote to him only once because, like many students, I had no fixed address and lost touch with him. I often wondered if he ever did get an education. All my university friends were from the border areas. If communication was difficult during times of peace, just imagine what it was like during times of war! There is a Chinese classic saying:

Water flows East from ancient times, Looks simple and easy, But is it really so?

Before we moved to Yao Pu, I went to bid good-bye to Ta-Sao's father, who was very stern, so I asked MC to go with me. When we reached their house, the bodyguard met us the door, showed us to the drawing room, and asked us to wait while he went to call his master. The venerable old man dressed in an old-fashioned long gown came through the curtained doorway. I stood up and bowed toward him in the Ching dynasty style. Though the revolution was already twenty years old and such ancient attire was out-of-date, they were still worn by some elders. I introduced MC, saying that he was a schoolmate and childhood friend of mine from XiKhang and that he had just returned from the northeast and was temporarily staying with my family. I also said that MC had helped us a lot during Hsueh GeeKow's funeral rites.

"Sit down. Sit down," said Ta-Sao's father, and as soon as we sat down, he continued, "Your father said that when GeeKow died, Ta-Sao had nowhere to go and had asked her to return home, so we fetched her." I was shocked to hear this as it had always been her idea that she should return home. In one sentence, he had placed the blame squarely on our shoulders. I was taken aback, but before I could utter a word, MC piped up sweetly, "Please, Uncle, may I say a few words from what I saw and heard regarding this matter?" Ying *BeiBei* (Ta-Sao's father) was surprised, hesitated, and replied, "hao, hao, hao, speak, speak, speak all you want."

MC began, "When I returned to Chengdu from the northeast, at first, I stayed in SayChing's house. Later, when they moved, it was too far from my office, so I moved to Hsueh Fourth Brother ChiPei's Elder Brother GeeKow's house. He had been transferred from Stone Bridge to Chengdu, so he asked Uncle Hsueh and his family to live with them too, though the house was a bit small for so many people."

"Yes, GeeKow had lived with you all at that time," said Ching (old man)

"I never thought GeeKow decided to move to YaoPu, but before he moved, he had discussed it with Auntie Hsueh that if her family were to live in his house, they were to pay fifty yuan a month. Then all will be satisfactory. I too moved with the Hsuehs, and I paid GeeKow twenty yuan a month. In fact, the Hsuehs paid sixty yuan a month, *not* fifty. GeeKow gave me receipts for all the payments, though, at that time, I had thought it was unnecessary. But he was very straightforward and meticulous and insisted, and I am glad to have those receipts now because they will clear up a lot of misunderstandings. When he died suddenly, the death responsibilities fell on Hsueh BeiBei, but he was not in Chengdu at that time, so all the responsibilities had fallen on Fourth Brother's young shoulders. He and I grew up together and are like blood brothers. As I am in Chengdu, I helped in any way I could. Today Uncle GeeKow is gone. Though his wife has a pension, which we have already forwarded to you, she also had great expenses. She cannot afford the house or take care of concubine-sister and the baby anymore, so it was *she* alone who decided to return to her family home with concubine-sister and baby. The Hsueh family did not send her away." MC finished and bowed with a flourish. Ching BeiBei looked slightly sheepish. He had nothing to say, so we bid him good-bye politely and left.

Alas, we all had to move again, this time to Tse Tung Road. The house had one large room, large enough for four people to stay, and a small room for MC and me. The middle room was for a shrine while next to our room was the kitchen. Alas, there was only one bathroom, which we all had to share.

Yi-Nyang and Her Daughter Leaves the Hsuehs

One day, while MC was talking with the landlord's brother, a successful businessman who had a Shanghainese wife who spoke in a different dialect, which we did not understand. Her husband was saying to us, "Nowadays, things are different. It is no longer customary for widows to remain unmarried. That is why your Yi-Nyan is thinking of leaving."

MC and I were surprised to hear this. I said, "The Hsueh family did not control her at all, only took care of the needs of her and her child. She could do what she wanted. She never told us that she wanted to leave. Let us ask her." We went to Mma first and asked her if she had heard anything about this. She and Yi-Nyang were standing in the front room and talking.

"Mma, is it true Yi-Nyang and her children are leaving?" I asked.

"Yes, they are leaving," Mma said.

"You have always taken care of me," said Yi-Nyang, "even during the days when I was unreasonable and intolerable. When my husband died, you could easily have thrown me out. Then where could we have gone? We could have jumped into a well, yet you kept us and looked after us. I will never forget your benevolence." So saying, she kowtowed in front of her husband's spiritual tablet and bowed toward Mma. She took Small Sister's hand and her boy in the other. They climbed into a rickshaw and left. I never saw them again.

Fang TsuTse—Line of Defense

At that time, Chengdu was separated into three defense districts, each with its own territory. Sao Cheng belonged to the Twenty-fourth Army, commanded by General Lin Weng Hwei; the Twenty-eighth Army under General Deng ScheeHu; and the Twenty-ninth Army under General Tien SongYao.

One day, at daybreak, our dreams were broken by loud bullet reports. We immediately dove under the table on top of which we piled blanket and quilts, thinking we would be safe from gunfire. We remained there until we could hear no more sounds. Gingerly, we emerged from under the tables and saw our landlord's new Shanghainese sister-in-law shivering and asking, "What's happened? What's happened, Aya? Are we going to die?"

"We don't know," I answered. "But we are going to find out."

MC and I opened the gate and went out. As soon as we opened the door, we heard a sound like cicadas, and a thing fell at MC's feet. He picked it up, which was a bullet from a rapid-fire machine gun. Fortunately, it had diffused. Otherwise, it could have been the end of my dear friend. If this was so, then the Japanese were on the ground not too far away.

MC said, "Let us not go out now. We had better wait awhile."

Next morning, at nine, we saw people walking about, so we then went to the end of our street to a little teashop to ask what had happened that night. There were two armed soldiers "protecting" the head of the street. We saw a group of people who had covered their heads with blankets and pillows, some carrying bundles and baskets, as if they were refugees, running away. A foreigner who was leading them told the soldiers that they were members and students of the Inland Christian Association. Their school was too near frontline, so under the leadership of their minister, they gathered as much of their possessions and ran to this safer location. Because he was a foreigner, the soldiers did not give him a hard time. Then we heard sounds of planes in the sky.

"Go quickly. The enemy planes are coming," shouted the soldiers.

The foreigner spoke Chinese in a peculiar accent, which made us laugh. "That is not your enemy. Your enemy is coming from the northeast [meaning the Japanese]."

The soldiers were astonished and turned to us, "What is he saying?"

We laughingly told them that we did not think it was true either.

Then one of the soldiers turned to the foreigner. "Go. Don't talk too much. Go quickly."

"Who are they?" we asked.

The soldiers did not know and would not say. Perhaps the foreigner was right after all: those were not enemy planes.

Alas, we had to move again, this time from Tsee Tung Street to East Tung Shung Street, close to our relatives, the Lee family. This family was my paternal uncle (i.e., his mother's brother) and also GeeKow's granduncle, who had died very young age, so Grand auntie had raised all six children herself. She was a capable and beautiful woman and had only one assistant, a servant girl, who had been one of Fourth Uncle's concubines. This girl had pockmarks and unbound feet; thus, she was called Big Foot, but she had a heart of gold and was a tremendous help to Great-Auntie. Her two hands were gifted. She could cook a delicious banquet in half a day, and her embroidery made the flowers and birds come alive; but because she was my fourth Great-Uncle's concubine, she was never able to marry, so she stayed with the family all her life. She took care of everyone as if we were her own family. During the New Year celebrations, she prepared three meals. First, there's breakfast of soft delicious lily roots and lotus seeds. If one were elderly, one had "golden cloud-ear mushrooms," or swallow's nest soup, and sometimes steamed sweet yellow or white cakes with tea. Two hours later, at 10:00 a.m., we had the main meal. Between about noon and 1:00 p.m., we had a snack called 'passing the noon' tasty soup. At about 4:30 p.m., we had our evening meal. At 9:00 p.m., we had our night snack, to pass the night, of noodles or something comforting. This schedule was true also for the office workers. We really only had two main meals a day; all the others were snacks. This tradition was carried on till WWII. It was only when I returned to Sichuan as a grown man and as manager of Pao Yuan Tung Trading Company did I learn that people had three main meals a day. By three meals, they meant three *solid* meals—rice was served even for breakfast. I could not stand this, so I had the kitchen change the breakfast to rice porridge, plus a few condiments of pickled vegetables, preserved eggs, and dried pulled pork. The employees were infuriated and complained loudly to me, "You are Sichuanese. How can you make us eat this watery rice? Only the people 'downstream' eat this weak stuff. Here, only the very poor and the very old toothless people eat this gruel, and even then, they only eat it behind closed doors!"

There was a reason for the laborers to prefer "dry rice." It was because of their hard physical work. The laborers said, "Even five bowls of water rice would not be enough." But despite their displeasure, I ordered the kitchen to continue to serve water rice for breakfast, but, the accompanying condiments grew more and more elaborate!

In China, during those days—and maybe even today, I do not know—most large companies' employees lived in compounds built for them, and all their room and board and other basic necessities like medical services and even primary schooling were taken care of by the employers.

The concubine at Great-Aunt's house was also an excellent cook, and whenever we visited Great-Aunt, and after all the formal greetings, she would tell us to "go and play." We would rush into the kitchen and ask Concubine Auntie if she had anything for us to snack.

"Nothing, only dog's feet," she teased. Then we would all pounce on her, some on her back. Some pulled her legs and arms, some tickled her.

"You are going to break me in half," she joked and pretended to cry. "Okay, okay, I'll give you some cats'ears to eat." (mao-erto) This was no joke. These were tiny cakes made of flour and which were something we could never tire. After half an hour, the "cats' ears" were brought out, tiny wonton made to look like the ears of cats. Even Great-Aunt was surprised. "How did you make so many in only half an hour?"

"No, not half an hour. I started to make them at seven this morning."

We children did not know how special these dishes were. We only knew they were delicious, and we loved them and were thrilled when we got what we requested. While we were eating, we heard a quiet, gentle voice from inside the kitchen.

"Don't eat so fast. There are more delicious snacks coming." We looked up and saw my mother's grandmother—Great-Grand-Mma to some, the oldest person in the house and the most revered—come into the kitchen. Every time Grandaunt ran out of money, she came to my mother to borrow some, and Grandaunt would say, "Again, I cannot manage." Mma would at once hand her twenty silver yuans without a word. Grandaunt would take it, also without a word.

Chapter 3

Leaving Home To Yuh Schen Or Nanking

Father's letter came to say that the local school lacked an English teacher and hoped that I would go and take up that job. If I had followed Baba's wishes, I would immediately have been united with my family and, thus, would have been able to help my mother with her expenses, my sister by taking her to the Yueh School, and other chores around the house. At first, it seemed like a good plan, but I had my doubts. First, I did not think my English was good enough to teach; and second, all my schoolmates had gone away for further studies and were working already. If I went to Yueh School, I would be going backward, and nothing may come of it. I may be going into a dead end. I was at a quandary, so I discussed this with my older and good friend MC. He told me that he felt he had made a mistake in returning to Sichuan and was even considering leaving again; therefore, he agreed with me that I should pursue higher studies. Meanwhile, I received a letter from ChungJuin, asking me to join him that summer in Nanking and take the Nanking University entrance examination, and I could stay with him. After much soul searching, I wrote a long and very clear letter to Baba, telling of my decision. He not only agreed but also sent me one hundred and twenty yuan for my journey and living expenses for the first four months. He added that since I had decided to go away to university, I should not worry about his health. From these few words, I deducted that his health was not good, but he did not prevent me from going, only encouraged me with these words: 'If Mother and Father are still alive, one should not go away. But if one must, then one should have a good and detailed plan and direction.' So began my journey to the outside world - away from my family, my boyhood friends, and familiar places. Mma asked MC who was a good ten years older than me to look after me, his little brother. Fighting back her tears, she said, "MungChow, you are a good deal older than ChiPei. He is a very good boy, but he tends to be too kind and tenderhearted sometimes, and people may take advantage of him. Look after him. He is your little brother."

Baba never said such words. This memory also returns to me from time to time, and I have often wondered that if I had not left, I would have been there to look after him when he became ill and may have not died so young. He was only fifty-three.

When two of my friends, Yang MungYu and HwaTsao, heard that MC and I were going to Nanking, they wanted to come with us. I was hesitant, but MC immediately agreed. Our route was palanquin from Chengdu, *hwa kang* (kind of wheelbarrow) to Shiaochi, boat to Lungchang, car to Chungking, and steamer along Tsang Jiang (Yangtse River) to Hankow and finally to Nanking. We decided the date of our departure.

Mma and Jiehjeih (elder sister) moved in with BaoTai (grandaunt), and we agreed on twenty silver yuan for their room and board, quite a good rate for the times. BaoTai often stayed with her second daughter, whose husband was a second-class warlord whom I had never seen. I only saw his photograph dressed as a general, but no matter how arrogant or efficient looking, I never felt comfortable for Mma and Jiehjieh to be living in that household. Only BaoTai's third and youngest daughter made me feel secure, and I felt that she would take care of Mma and Jiehjieh.

Before I left, I went to kowtow to Mma. She held me and cried, "Aya, Baobei [precious one], you must take care of yourself. When cold, put on a coat. Remember, don't forget to eat [which I used to do when I was involved in something]. When you have time, write home often, but don't write too *tsaow* [running script] because your sister will not be able to read the letters then."

I smiled and said, "Eighth Auntie is a good person. If there is anything you need, tell her.

This time, when we moved to BaoTai's house, except for BaoTai herself, Great-Auntie and the others were happy to receive us," said Mma.

"Why was BaoTai unhappy?" I asked.

"That is not exactly the case. As long as your father sends the monthly rent, she cannot be unhappy. Also, the Tenth Uncle and his wife and concubine will all look after us."

I tried hard to extract myself from Mma's arms and pulled away. Jiehjieh and I looked at each other for a moment; then tearfully, without another word, I turned and rushed out of the door without looking back. I never saw my sister again and never was able to find her when China opened for tourists half a century later.

MungChow cried out, "Auntie, go indoors. Third Sister, take Auntie by the hand."

MC and I quickly went out of the East Gate and across the SceeMa Bridge. During the times of the Three Warring Kingdoms, ChuKuo KungMing sent ChangFei to the Kingdom of Wu, and this was the bridge he and his soldiers had to cross.

KungMing had said, "One thousand li [Chinese mile] journey to Jin Ning starts from here."

Now, more than a millennia later, I was about to cross the same bridge. The very idea made me proud to be part of that history. These one thousand years have passed like a dream, and I have come to this point to be part of the continuation of that dream. My head twirled around like a confused sky before a thunderstorm, and as I stood on the bridge, I heard an impatient cry from the palanquin bearer,

"Hey, are you coming into the palanquin, or are you walking?"

I was pulled out of my reverie. HwaTsao and Yang MungYu were already waiting for us. We climbed into the palanquin and went to the JinMing marketplace. We then negotiated the price for the next leg of our complicated journey: boat to Lungchan.

Ningkiang Scee's Bean Sauce

We arrived at Ningkiang, a small market town along the YangTse River. After taking our luggage to the hotel, we went to the marketplace to see what was there. Though only a small town, there were many streets with numerous shops busy and bustling with customers. It was said that the famous bean sauce originated here. We immediately bought two cans of this sauce to take to Nanking for our friends.

Next morning, at daybreak, we hurried over to the docks to board our sailing vessel (junk). Two persons rowed in the front, and at the back, the owner/captain worked the rudder. He addressed us, "You young men and women are lucky. The wind is behind us today, so we will be able to reach Lungchan in the afternoon. Do you know that Chungchan produces linen, Yuchan sugar, and FuSwen salt? All these come from the general area of Lungchan. I can let you stay there for a little while for you to look around and 'play' [Chinese idiom for 'to have fun']."

"Thank you, but we must get to Chungking," said MC.

"Oh," exclaimed the captain, so he ordered for the sails to be unfurled. As we drifted away from the shore, gradually, Ningkiang became obscured as if by a curtain of smoke.

Suddenly, we saw a red line across the sky, which became a fiery ball. The waves in the water turned to gold, and the red ball rose from the golden waters. We were breathless as we watched in wonder, and I was reminded of the words of the poet Bei LoTien:

Red sun rises from the scarlet river flowers. In spring, water clear as green hue.

I had had no experience of Jiangnan, but now I know it was truely beautiful. The smell of cooking meat wafted toward us, and turning our heads, we saw the captain carrying a small saucepan full of boiled beef and turnips.

"It is half a day now. You must be hungry. Come and eat something."

Following him, we saw a small barrel of white rice, a large plate of whitish coarse powder, a bowl of chili oil, and plate of cooked beef strips and slivers of raw turnips.

"Where is the salt?" we asked.

"This here is the salt."

"Oh, we did not know that this is the salt," we replied.

We piled our bowls with rice and took mouthfuls of beef dipped in the chili oil and the coarse salt. It was the most delicious and simplest meal I had ever eaten. We thanked the captain, and by noon, we had arrived. We gave him one yuan for the meal. He wished us good luck and sailed away.

River and Road Confluence

When we arrived at the rather large dock at Luchang, we went into a teashop at the dockside, and as soon as we sat down, a man came and asked us, "Where are you all going? Yuingchang, Kangjin, or Chungking?"

"Is there a car going to Chungking?" we asked.

"Oh, you four want to go to Chungking? That is easy. You can rent a car now, and by five in the afternoon, you will arrive in Chungking."

We had no idea that it would be so quick, so we rented a car; and accordingly, we reached Chungking. MC took us to see his uncle, Mr. BeiYi, who was a famous acupuncturist and herbalist doctor. When we arrived, it was very hot; by the time we reached his front door, we were all perspiring and uncomfortable. His house was very big and impressive. We were led to his chambers, which was in fact a big hall surrounded by all manner of patients—women, men, young, and old. We saw a very fat fellow without any shirt on, sitting facing and talking to a young girl.

MC called, "Uncle Number One."

The fat man turned around and boomed, "Aha, Number Three, did you not go northwest to Manchukuo [Manchuria]?"

"Uncle, I returned from the NW almost a year ago, and I am about to return to Nanking."

"Nanking, eh? Have you worked there before?"

"Yes," said MC, "and also I am taking my friends there too," pointing to me and my two friends. "This is Hsueh Chi Pei. We were in primary school together."

Uncle BeiYi rushed over to me and took my hand and shook it. His palm was huge and soft, and I felt as if my own hands were enveloped in a large piece of fatty meat. "And this is Yang MungYu and HwaTsao, whom I met in Chengdu."

"Today you are not allowed to leave. You must dine with me," he exclaimed.

"No, no, we must go catch our boat to Nanking," MC protested.

"No," he insisted, "you may not go. After dinner, I will give you some medicine to take with you, which you are bound to find useful in Nanking."

As he was saying this, his assistant came and announced, "Sir, your friend, the consulate general of France, wants to see you."

"Show him in."

In walked a foreigner holding his head. He said in perfect Mandarin, "It's hurting. My head is hurting me to death!"

I was astonished that this foreigner could speak such good Chinese and was also Uncle BeiYu's friend.

"So," Uncle BeiYu said, "trust you are not dead."

"If I were really dead, I would not be able to speak."

Everyone laughed. Even the consulate general started to laugh at his own joke despite his headache.

"Stop talking rubbish." He pretended to be in agony.

Uncle BeiYu sat him on a stool and took a three-inch-long golden needle like a hairpin and pushed it obliquely into the foreigner's scalp and twirled it a bit. Bei *Daifu* (Bei doctor) then addressed the consulate general softly, "Cramping?"

"Cramping, cramping, aw, aw, aw," replied the Frenchman.

We did not know what all this meant. Bei Daifu twirled the needle again. The foreigner shouted, "Oh, how hot, how hot!" Perspiration began to drop down his head like running water, and in about half an hour, his entire body was soaked.

Bei Daifu then removed the needle. Not a drop of blood was shed. "Hao la [okay]," said BeiDaifu. The consulate general took a couple of deep breaths then stood up and looked at Bei Daifu.

"You are truly my life saver." Then turning to all of us, he said, "With such a doctor, of what illness could you be afraid?"

Bei Daifu then admonished, "Go away. Don't talk such nonsense. Now no wine for six months."

"How can that be? In my line of work, we must 'wine and dine' guests all the time. Furthermore, I am French. I cannot survive without wine!"

"How is it, sir, with so much learned Chinese scholarship, you do not know the well-known Chinese saying:

'If guests arrived during a cold winter's night, serve tea instead of wine'?"

The French consulate laughed and said, "You are an impossible man." He had been relieved of his severe headache and left a very happy man indeed. We, meanwhile, could not stay as we had a boat to catch.

We had reservations on a boat run by the Ming Shipping Company, which was solely owned by the Ming family. When we boarded the steamer, we came across cousin GeeKow's adopted daughter, Hung Kwan, and her PhD American husband and his mother. They were ahead of us in the queue, but they were going first class while we students were going down below to the "cattle yard" (third class). Hung Kwan saw me and whispered something to her mother-in-law. We quickly took our places and pretended we did not see them. Later, we saw them several times, but they pretended that they did not know us. MC said to me, "Why are you so stubborn? So what, if you greeted them a little?"

"Why should I?" I replied. "If they don't want to recognize us, then why force them? We are not going to the same place anyway."

Wu-Xia Beido Cheng Foon Du (Wu-Xia Gorge)

There were no assigned seating in the third-class level of the steamer, so we had to struggle to find good places. Out of the three gorges, Wu-Xia is the longest. Hearing the cries of the monkeys brought tears to my eyes. I had told myself over and over that I must not be asleep when we pass this place, so when we arrived, I heard nothing but thought and remembered the poem:

I said good-bye to Bei DiCheng still among the clouds.

One thousand li to Chieng LieIng takes only one day.

On both shores, monkeys' cries never stop.

The night boat crossed over one thousand layers of mountains.

I wanted to ask someone about these lines, but we had already arrived at our destination, and the moment had passed.

ChangJiang (Yangtse River) steamers went from Hankow to Shanghai, stopping on the way at JuChinang, where we had to change boats to continue our journey to Nanking. We stepped from one boat to the other without even setting foot on the ground. On this second boat, we quickly "bagged" our space, i.e., put our bags down, before going ashore to explore. (In those days, people were honest because it never entered our young minds that someone may steal our bags.) We went to the docks where I saw a man balancing a basket of huge bunches of long yellow fruits. He was calling out to buyers, "Come buy my sweet bananas. Fifty cents. Only fifty cents a bunch!"

I had read about and seen pictures of them in my books as a child, but I had never eaten one myself or seen anyone else eat them. I was curious, so I spent fifty cents and bought a bunch. I took one of the long yellow fruits, which looked delicious, so I bit into it. It was awful, bitter, extremely fibrous, and totally puckered up my mouth. In disgust, I threw the entire bunch into the river. I had never eaten anything so horrid like it before; it was the worst fruit I had ever tasted. Beside me, a young man, who also looked like a university student, sighed and shook his head.

"What a pity. What a waste of a good bunch of bananas. What ignorance."

I said irritably, "I was cheated. The man who sold them to me said that they were very ripe and sweet. This bunch was not ripe at all. How could he sell them and cheat people?"

"Ha-ha, you did not peel it, did you?" he asked disdainfully.

"What? Do you mean you have to peel the banana?" I began to feel really stupid.

"Have you never eaten a banana before?"

"No," I replied, "they don't grow where I come from, but I have read about them and seen pictures of them in books. No one ever mentioned that they had to be peeled to be eaten."

"No wonder. I am also from Chengdu and did not see a banana until I went to Beijing." We soon became friends, and I learned that he had not only been cousin GeeKow's colleague but was also a grandson of one of my previous English teachers in Chengdu. When we arrived in Nanking, we said good-bye as he had to take the Jing *TiehLu* (iron road, i.e., train) to Beijing.

We also said good-bye to Yang MungYu and HwaTsao while MC and I went to the Sikhang People's Republic representative's office to see our friends Ma ChehTsow, the head of the office; Cheng ChenChuan; and his deputies Yang ShienTse and Shen ShankWie. They used to call me *masculeh* (tadpole) because I was the youngest and most active one. I found that the big city had not changed them at all, except that Ma ChehTsow had become quite fat. I jokingly said, "Hey, you have become like a fat pig," which was very impolite because I had forgotten that he was a Muslim. Had we not been very good old friends, I should not have taken such liberties.

He retorted, "Hey, masculeh, you are no longer a child. You must improve your manners. I am not angry with you because we have known

136

each other for a long time, and I know you are not being deliberately rude, but there are Muslims here, and they will not take kindly to these kinds of jokes."

I apologized immediately and said that I had forgotten that he was a Muslim. I have always been very grateful to his advice, and except for coming across him occasionally during our studies or at work, I hardly ever met him. The last time I saw him was at his arrest. One day I saw a large crowd gather in the marketplace, and when I went closer to see what was going on, to my horror, I saw an old acquaintance. He had been arrested for bribery at his work and was due to be executed by gunfire by the Twenty-fourth Army. To my mind, if he were to be executed for bribery, how many hundreds of others would have and should have suffered the same fate? I thought that there must have been more to it than what appeared. This man had been sent to Sikhang from Beijing under orders from higher up, so I was sure he opposed the local government there and had done something that eventually caused his demise. I had lost an excellent friend of my youth.

Hung TseLung's Yu-Tiao (Fried Bread Sticks)

One of the students I had met on the way had told us that we had to rise early in the morning to go to Hung TseLung's stall to buy his *yu-tiao* (fried bread sticks) before we went to take our entrance examination. MC woke first then woke up the rest of us. Hung's shop was directly opposite the school, so I went to it and bought a bowl of soya-bean milk and two pieces of yu-tiao. Just as I was about to eat, MC rushed out of the school and shouted, "Stop eating. It is time."

I put down my breakfast and ran to the classroom. I saw that many students were seated, brushes in hand, and were ready. The topic of the examination was already on the blackboard. We were asked to write an essay relating to our experience from our home village to Nanking. In the classroom, there was a man who might have been both the professor and the invigilator. The silence in the hall was deafening. Because we used Chinese brushes, there was not even the sound of pen or pencil scratches. After more than three hours, I finished and came out of the examination hall to see MC waiting for me.

"Well, so how was it? What is the result?"

"I don't know yet."

"Anyway, don't think about it. Let us go and eat lunch. You missed breakfast."

At the meal, I asked, "What happened to WangTsow? Why did he not show up?"

"There was a problem, or maybe the XiKhang representative officer will send him later," MC replied. I did not understand what he had meant. WangTsow was from XiZhang, but in any case, what was the difference between XiZhang and XiKhang? They were both border areas. YangYu started to explain, but MC interrupted, "I will explain it to you one day." But he never got a chance.

One Sunday, ChungJuin, my best friend from Lucheng, came into town from Hsio Tswang, which is now part of the university campus.

"At last you have come out," he exclaimed, meaning coming out of the remote border areas, beaming with joy. He wanted me to go with him to HsioTswang. I asked my supervisor Ma ChungBung's permission.

"Of course, you should. ChungJuin is your childhood friend, and it is good to keep such friendships."

Then I took my simple belongings and went with ChungJuin. Everyone was happy for me, except MC. When I arrived at HsioTswang, I saw all my classmates from Lucheng, and we all greeted one another with great delight. One of them came up to me and slapped me on the shoulders and cried, "Hsueh, you snow pig [*Hsueh* sounds like *snow* phonetically, and snow pigs were very small pigs that hide in caves during the winter, and their meat was particularly delicious], why did it take you so long to come out? We could have all graduated next year and then returned home and started our own schools or done something together."

"Earthly god," I said (I called him that because he was dark and small), "my father had been posted to the far border areas. I had to arrange for my mother and sister to live with some relatives so that they will be looked after when I left them. It was only when my father returned that I felt able to come."

Just as we were in the depth of our conversation, ChungJuin came and announced, "Dinnertime."

Since the school term had not yet started, the dining hall was rather empty, and the food was not appetizing. We merely looked in and left. That night I slept on the bunk above ChungJuin. Another student used to sleep in ChungJuin's bunk. That young man used to jump into the Yangtse River from Yieng Tse Rock—a brave but foolish thing to do—because he wanted to show that he was a good swimmer and was not afraid of either the height from which he jumped or the currents of the river. However, once, he caught a very bad cold and could not shake it off, so he went home to recuperate, but he never returned because he had died of pneumonia.

I stayed at the university to prepare for my studies. MC was upset that I did not assist him to help Yang MungYu and WangTsow settle at the university. A week later, we received our school entrance notices. It was only after entering the college, did we realize that, except for classroom instructions, everything else was structured on the military style. In actual fact, it was really a war college. We arose at six every morning, and five minutes later, we had to assemble in the field to raise the Kuomintang flag (Nationalist). Then we started the morning exercises until 7:30 a.m., after which, we were allowed to have breakfast in the dining hall. Classes started at 8:00 a.m. All these different schedules were clearly demarcated by the sound of bugles. At first, we found this regimen very taxing, especially for us students from the border areas where we were used to a certain amount of freedom, but we had to get used to it.

Hsio Tswang at the Foothills of MoFu Shan

During the Ching dynasty, Hsio Tswang was a very famous place, and the atmosphere was noble and powerful. There was a modern school started by a certain Tao TseChing, who later changed it to Tao ChingTse. This man later built another primary school called Yieng TseGee Elementary School. I never saw either of these schools, but I did hear that

"The sound of wind in the pine trees on MoFu Hill was like large waves playing on the Yieng Tse rocky cliff."

This cliff jutted tens of feet out over the Yangtse River and was the rock off which JuinChung's bunkmate used to jump. One day two schoolmates from Mongolia and I were walking from MoFu Hill to the San Tai Cave, where a famous monk of olden times was supposed to have lived. We decided to take a shortcut behind our school to the cave. We had been walking about half an hour when we saw a cannon on a platform.

My Mongolian friend cried, "This cannon must be at least one hundred years old, made during the war of 1850–1864, between Cheng KueChuang and See TaKai, at the time of the Heavenly Kingdom of Peace, which was founded by Hung HsiuChuang, when the capital at that time was Nanking. Possession of this area gave control of the right bank of the Yangtse River."

Before I could respond, we were startled by an enormous sound as if one thousand horses were bearing down upon us. We cowered and were dumbstruck; simultaneously, a sudden wind blew through the pine trees, making sounds like hundreds of monkeys screeching and devils dancing. Now I understood the meaning of "pine waves."

It took us over an hour to walk from MoFu Hill to the edge of the river. We passed the Tou Tau Cave and finally to the YiengTse Gee cliff, which projected over what seemed like into the middle of the river. On the opposite bank was the Pa Kwa Chow (district), a borderless wilderness. Looking down, people looked like ants and the boats like small grains of peas. The cliff suspended over the water as if it would fall in. No wonder star-crossed lovers and unsuccessful businessmen chose this spot to jump in and end their lives. We discovered that the Lola Fuaukitu monk from Sizhang (Tibet) had carved these words "Ohm Mani Padme Hum" in Tibetan. Maybe he carved them to try to change the minds of would-be suicide victims, but it would be like holding a horse back at the final moment of victory. He must have not known Chinese, so he had carved the words in Tibetan, or perhaps he had felt that the Tibetan language would be more effective. I am sure he did not carve those words for his own glorification. Most of the people who came from Tibet or SiKhang were mostly businessmen and would not have bothered to climb all this way, or if they did, they probably did not understand the words either. So, did the monk carve them for the people from Nanking who did not know Tibetan? Who did he carve them for? While I was standing at the edge, pondering, my friends called out to me,

"Hey, what are you thinking about? Are you going to commit suicide?"

I laughed and told them what I was pondering about.

"That is nothing. Any lama could have carved those words. Our monks are forever chanting 'Oh me to Fu.' So why should not a lama carve 'ohm mani padme hum' in his own language?"

Then I asked, "Do you understand what these words mean?"

"No," he replied.

"It means 'the leaves of the lotus arise from the heart of the lotus.'"

He looked puzzled and said, "I do not understand."

"If one were to really explain the meaning of these words, it would take ages. The lamas said that it would take eight hours a day for three months to fully explain the true meaning of those words."

He was astonished and said impatiently, "Never mind, never mind, it is enough for me. If you suggest that I go to a real lama and listen, I will certainly go mad."

Then we looked into the San Tai Cave near the carved stone, where the lama was supposed to have lived. We looked into this cave; and in the dark gloom, we saw the preserved body of the lama, seated in a full lotus position, enshrouded in a gold habit. It has been mystery to me how that dead lama could have sat there, so upright, for all those years, and no one has ever mentioned him. I dared not touch it for fear that he would crumble if I did. We gazed at it for a long time in silence, unable to believe what we saw, and silently crept out of the cave. I cannot now recall the lama's name as I was not really interested in that particular sect. When we came out of the cave and headed back to school, we walked through luxuriant growth of brilliant magenta-colored pomegranate blossoms, which covered the entire hillside. My friends and I wandered about still in silence, totally enchanted by the beauty of the place and the miracle we had just witnessed. We almost forgot that we had to be back in school by 4:00 p.m. Otherwise, we would not be allowed to go out again by ourselves.

WuYu Lane

The office of the Sikhang People's representative was located on WuYu Lane, which, historically, used to be a lane of great beauty. It was known even in AD 600 during the Tang dynasty, and a poem had been written about this particular lane:

Around ChuCho Bridge, wild flowers and grass abound,

Entrance of WuLu Lane the sun never sets,

Ancient Wang and Hsieh swallows fly about their halls,

Now fly away to common people's modest homes.

I had often wanted to see for myself this famous lane; and since, as the editor of our school magazine, I had to go to our school printing press every Sunday to edit and print our magazine, I decided to go and see this spot for myself before classes officially started. Sadly, what I found was disgusting. On one side of the street, instead of wild grasses, an unkempt public toilet and, on the other side, instead of fragrant pomegranate flowers, the stench of refuse filled the air. Alas, is this the idea of progress?

I asked my friend Ma TseTsow, who lived near there. "How can you live in this dirty place?"

"I have no choice." He replied, this is only a few minutes' walk from my office. If I were to live further away, I would have to spend too much money going back and forth on the bus. I cannot afford that."

At a distance from Wu-Lu Lane was a street from which wafted wave after wave of a foul odor, which pierced right through my brain and made me want to vomit but at the same time gave me a sensation of great lethargy. We walked as fast as we could away from this place. We discovered that the smell came from a street stall where something was being fried. I dared not stop, so I pinched my nose and ran quickly through WuLu Lane. At a distance, we saw a small bridge, which must be the "Chu Chuo Bridge of the swallows" mentioned in the Tang poem. Here, too, there were no flowers. Ma Cheh Tsow said, noticing my expression of disgust at the strange and unpleasant smell,

"That smell comes from frying the 'swallow tofu,' the euphemistic name for 'smelly tofu,' the most precious thing of the Nanking people. If you cannot bear that smell, then, you must go around this area and come via Swui Shee Meng, past the Ching Hwai House of Wine." He then smiled. From then on, that was the way I always took. I could not appreciate Nanking's famous "smelly tofu" as it was called.

Lady of the Boats

Whoever had read the Tang poems must have come across TuMu's lines:

Anchoring at Ching Hwai House at night, Smoke covers the cold stream, Gauze shrouded the full moon. Anchor at night at Ching Hwai House, The ladies there know not the sorrow of kings. Beyond the river still sings Hou Ting Wha tunes.

While I was at the university, I had neither the time nor the means to visit such houses of "pleasure women"; and if we were discovered, we would have been expelled. However, when I graduated, I wanted to go and see, like all forbidden fruits, what went on there. I thought to myself, *After all, what harm could there be just looking?*

I went to Fu Tse Temple, walking slowly along the riverbank toward Ching Hwai House. I saw many sampans docked alongside the boardwalk; each of these little boats carried four to five people. I waited for a while but saw neither "smoke-covered stream" nor the "gauze-enshrouded moon." I only felt wafts of bad smell come into my nostrils and thought someone was defecating into the river, so to avoid being splashed, I jumped into one of those sampans. Out of nowhere, the owner of the boat suddenly materialized and sidled up to me and said, "Shall I send a note?"

"Can you row the boat to the next exit?" I asked. His face was full of astonishment.

"What? Go out, exit? What do you mean? There are only a few small openings on this river, and they are all blocked. No way out anywhere."

"Then how can I get out of here? How can the Ching Hwai boat people bear this awful stench? How can you live here?"

"Hey, no, that is not the point. The people who come to these boats come here only to find a girl and spend some time on the boats. They do not come here to go anywhere or to experience the beauties of nature." The boat owner looked at me as if I had just emerged from the countryside villages (which, as a matter of fact, I did, not too long ago). "So, sir," he explained to me, "when you first jumped into my boat, I had asked you if you wanted me to send you a note. You said that you wanted to go out, that you wanted to take a boat ride on this river. That business, sir, is in Hungchow's West Lake. We do not do that business here. Let me tell you, since you, obviously, are new to this 'wind.' All you do is simply call for a girl to keep you company for a while."

"Oh, you mean a prostitute?" I blurted. Though I had never seen or met one, I knew what those "girls" were called. I asked awkwardly, "How much will she cost?"

The boat owner laughed and said, "Not very much, only one to five yuans according to your generosity, but the boat itself costs three yuans. Okay, let me call a girl for you, one who has some education. Simply give her one or two or three yuans. It will be sufficient." "Will she be able to talk to me?" I asked.

"If she understands you, why would she not be able to answer, eh?" He then called out. His assistant was already on his way to find a girl for me.

Not more than two minutes later, another boat came alongside our boat, and from there emerged a girl dressed like a student: short navy blue pleated skirt and a white blouse. Her long hair was done in two braids with a little bow at each end. I saw that she was not as young as she was dressed, most probably even several years older than I. She came and sat down on my left and right away put her right thigh on mine before I had even asked her name. I was taken aback and immediately stood up and said,

"Miss, what is your name?"

Impatiently, she answered, "Ching Chui." (*Ching* means *gold* and *chui*, *autumn*.) *A rather poetic name*, I thought, but I was most disappointed when she explained the real intended meaning of chui was "to want money."

"I hear miss has been to school," I said. "Which school?"

"That was the school near my house, but it is closed now," she replied rudely.

"Is there anyone else in your honorable home?" I tried again to be polite.

She did not speak to me again but turned to the boat owner and started to talk to him. I could not talk to her anymore either. I gave the owner three yuans for his boat. "Three yuans for the 'note' and three yuans to the girl," I said and started to get off the boat. The owner looked embarrassed and said, "Sir, sorry, you have spent so much for nothing."

"That's enough," I said. "You have taught me things of which I knew nothing about. This girl may be rude, but she seems to be quite straightforward and maybe quite nice. She is just doing her job."

Then the girl came up to me and knelt before me. Full of tears, she apologized and said, "Yesterday a government official came to me and started to ask me about my family conditions too. I have no one at home. My sister and brothers are all scattered. That official was not only unsympathetic but suspected that I had undeclared taxable income! He had told me that he would send a tax collector to come and inspect me. Today, when I saw you, I thought that you were that man. I had wanted to flatter you, but when I found sir was so formal and stiff and would not respond, I decided to pull away. I was terribly wrong, and I have offended a good man. Please forgive me." I then pulled her up and gave her two more yuans. She did not want to accept it, but the boatman exclaimed,

"Aya, this is a good man. He is giving you good money. It is difficult to get 'honest' money these days. You cannot even understand this little thing. Stop refusing. Take the kind gentleman's money. You don't even have this little bit of good manners. You poor thing."

Ching Chui then cried out aloud, "I understand, I understand. Thank you for teaching me." She accepted the money and asked, "What is your honorable sir's name? When were you born? Tell me, I will go to the temple and pray for you to have a long life without care."

I smiled. "Miss Ching Chui, I thank you for your kind intentions. I am giving you the money freely. I really have no other way to help you.

This little bit of money is only a token of my wishes. Do not worry too much. If you really believe heaven, then write or draw a picture of Kuan Yin Pusa and hang it up and pray, 'Lami ju kee, ju nan kwan scee yin pusa.'"

She bowed, kowtowed, and said, "I will do, will do."

The boat owner saluted me and said, "Don't forget us. If you are here again, I will invite you to eat Nanking's famous small soup dumplings and 'chou-tofu.'"

That awful smell I had just experienced not too long ago and from which I had run. I nodded, turned, and left. Somewhere, I could hear someone singing.

YiangTse Well (Lipstick)

I went to visit a Tibetan schoolmate called Dorji. He had come to Nanking from Kalimpong, a small border town in the foot of the Eastern Himalayas in India. He did not know Han Chinese, so he had to stay in a Han language tutorial school to learn Chinese first. This was a branch of the middle school of the Central University at TseJin Mountain, also called Chiang San, which was near the examination hall.

When I arrived, he said to me, "How are you?" in Chinese.

"You clever fellow, how quickly you have picked up Chinese." I was indeed surprised. He then continued in a long string of pure jargon, and I realized that aside from "How are you?" he did not know any more Chinese. He was quite distraught that his only friend, Tshi Jung, could speak both Chinese and Hwang Muslim. This Tashi Jung, formally the chief minister of Mongolia and the Tibetan Association, had been transferred to Lhasa, and I happened to be the only person who could communicate with him. All the other Tibetan students spoke Chinese well but did not take any notice of him.

Then I asked Dorji, "Now that you are here, did you know that this school has a well called Lipstick Well? Do you know where it is?"

"No, I do not, but there is a teacher here who is very helpful, and he may be able to tell you."

"Okay, take me to see him." He took me to the office of that teacher, who looked between forty and fifty years. I told him that I would like to see the school's famous Yiengtse Jing (Lipstick Well).

He did not seem surprised when I asked him, "Ah, you students from the border areas all know about this ancient story of Nanking. If you want to see it, then I will take you to it, but do you know the story of why it is called by that name?"

"Not too clear," I replied.

He related, "The story began about fourteen or fifteen hundred years ago, at the time of Chen HouJu, the last emperor of the Chen dynasty. Yang Kwang, the opposing general, had defeated Emperor Chen HouJu and started to storm the palace. The emperor had no time to escape, so he placed himself, his favorite concubine Kou PinFei, and Empress Chang LeeHwa into a basket and told his attendants to lower them into the dry well in the inner garden. Yang Kwang and his soldiers charged into the palace and looked everywhere for Emperor Chen HouJu, but he was nowhere to be found. When they came into the garden and saw the well, one of the soldiers shouted, 'Hey, let us throw some stones into this dry well so that it will never be used again.' The emperor shouted from the bottom of the well, 'No, no, stop.' The soldiers looked down and saw the emperor. The basket was pulled up slowly because it was much heavier than expected, and when it was brought to the surface, they saw that the emperor was not alone. They found his wife and concubine with him. The soldiers burst out laughing, and as the emperor started to climb out of the basket, it began to sway. This terrified Empress Chang LeeHwa, so she held on to the rim of the well with her mouth to steady the basket and, in doing so, left an imprint of her lipstick. Ever since that time, this well became the Yiengtse Jing."

This was a sad and touching story, a reminder of ancient times. When we went to what was the garden of the palace of Emperor Chen HouJu, the only thing standing was the well, but it was covered with a large wooden plank. Bare ground had replaced the ornamental pathways; the flowering trees and shrubs were no longer there. There were no garden seats to rest one's weary feet, and the surrounding palace buildings were replaced by concrete blocks of classrooms. It was sad that aesthetics had to give way to utilitarianism. Why cannot they exist side by side? It is a question I have asked myself time and time again. We wandered about a little in the space that was once the beautiful garden, and I imagined what it must have been.

Chapter 4

MUNG CHOW IN NANTUNG

I had wanted to visit Mung Chow in Nantung, but there were no rail connections between Nanking and Nantung although there was a road between the two cities, so we had to circumvent and travel north of Soubei (north of Chiangsoo), which was a very long way around. There was a shortcut if one went by the Ching Liang steamer, but even this boat did not dock at Nantung. It simply stopped in midstream, and smaller boats had to ply back and forth between the steamer and the shore. It was most frustrating and inefficient. The small boat docked at a small village not too far from the town of Nantung. I found a rickshaw and asked the man if he knew Tien Nin Scene.

"Of course, who doesn't know Tien Nin Scene?" I was delighted, and he then continued, "Nantung has thirteen areas. All have rickshaws, which is the main way people travel here and there. Communications are very easy, and we even have inter-area rickshaws, except for Area Five, in the south."

I thought to myself this is indeed a large district. The rickshaw people seemed to have cornered the market for travelers.

He continued, "Nantung is not only large, but it is also famous for its manufacture of yarn."

In a short while, we arrived in Tien Nin Scene, directly in front of MC's house; and at that very moment, he came out, saw me, and exclaimed, "I was just thinking as to how I was going to fetch you from Nanking."

At that time, MC was the chief of the Department of Opium Prohibition League; and later, when I graduated from university, I became one of his assistants. It was not that it was illegal for the addicts to smoke but that it was mandatory for them to register as addicts with this League; only then could they buy opium from certain government-licensed agencies. These offices were the Official Opium Suppliers. They were inspected, unannounced, by government officials three or four times a week.

When I started working there with MC, I found it very interesting. The addicts, at first, were considered patients with an illness and were given a chance to break the habit. However, if they were unable to do so after the allotted time, they were then considered criminals and had to give up the habit by force, or they were executed. It seemed harsh, but MC said that this was the only way to frighten the other addicts to quit their lazy and life-destroying habit.

I was often sent to inspect these shops. The licensed shop owners had to give a numerical account of the number of each packet by weight, which varied between one to five ounces. After inspecting them for the proper weight and purity, a government seal was stamped on each packet. There were many opportunities for corruption because of the collaboration between the inspectors and the shopkeepers. For instance, unsealed packets could be undeclared merchandise and, therefore, escaped being taxed; the amount in each packet could be tampered with after inspection; the number of packets could be falsified, etc. The ensuing moneys exchanged were shared between the guilty parties. Since I was new and totally innocent about such "arrangements," I was always the one being sent to inspect.

The addicts were required to register because every addict, after three months, had to give up smoking and check himself into a government opium "detox" institution under strict medical supervision. These addicts, would be arrested if they did not turn up. Some addicts escaped from these institutions, which only gave the government the right to arrest and incarcerate them into "detox" internment prisons. It was here that my future wife, ChowHsu, had worked. Here, the addict would no longer be considered only an "addict"; he was then called an addict-offense person. Heavy and frequent offenders were sometimes executed, and for the lighter offenders, they were sentenced to three years in jail and had to detox without any help—cold turkey.

I encountered a very difficult situation during one of my inspections. I had gone to the jail to check on the conditions there. A prisoner addict nicked named ShanHu (Third Mountain Tiger) was about to be executed.

He knelt before me, grabbed my legs, and begged me to save his life. "I have an eighty-year-old mother at home alone. If I die, who will look after her? She will surely die also."

"Rise," I said. "I don't know what I can do for you. I am new here and have no authority. My job is only to examine the living conditions of the inmates, whether all the prisoner addicts are fed properly and treated well, etc. As for who is a light or who is a heavy offender, I really have no say. But I do believe you when you say that you have an old mother at home living alone, and I will do what I can to help her. Also, whatever the law permits, I will do what I can to help the other addict inmates too."

At this moment, the prison guard shouted, "ShanHu, stop complaining and stop listening to that young commissioner." I realized that this guard's words were as much for me as for ShanHu. He did not like the way I was treating the inmates—with kindness and compassion. I pretended that I did not understand and left to see Judge Chang and asked him to help ShanHu. Justice Chang took his file and said, "I have just examined this case. The governor has already sentenced him."

"Ah," I said, "so it is done."

"What do you mean by that?" he asked.

I told him what had happened in the prison, and at the moment, MC came in and said, "The prison guard said that you are too soft and gentle. These prisoners think you are some kind of God. This attitude is not correct for them."

I retorted, "Let us not argue. I have already explained the situation to the judge."

Justice Chang then said, "What Mr. Wong MungChow said is right. According to the law, the jail guard is only doing his duty, though there is no need for him to be so harsh. Actually," the judge continued, "the law can only correct what is visible to the naked eye, but only one's conscience can help a person change his ways. The law deals with the branches of a tree, but the conscience takes care of the roots. Law is my profession. I can only follow that which is legal. I have no time to take care of the 'other' kind. ShanHu had broken the law many times, and according to the law, he should be executed this time. But he hugged your legs and begged you to forgive and help him because he must take care of his old mother. It is your conscience that has judged. Even his own mother had told him that what he was doing was wrong and against the law and that he should stop this habit. He did not even listen to her. So, I have no choice but to act according to the predicts of the law."

At this point, I shouted in anger, "His plea is that he wanted to help his old, helpless, and widowed mother. What I want to know is, should we not educate these poor people about the pitfalls of opium? According to our conscience and according to the people's 'right to life,' do you think we can be at peace with our own conscience, or do you think we have educated them enough?"

MC pointing at me, smirking, said, "He is angry. Look, look how mad he is. The governor had already given the order, so now there is only one path to follow, and that is, we must show 'them' we must follow orders."

The judge said, "Right, you carry it out."

MC then said, "Yes, the sooner the better. If delayed, there may be problem."

Reluctantly, I added, "All the prisoners are sympathetic toward SanHu."

"That is certain," said Judge Chang.

Then SanHu was led away and the orders carried out. I went out and saw a large crowd had gathered as if they were looking at a show in the marketplace. I could only feel Ko SanHu's arms around my legs and thought of his poor mother waiting for him to come home.

Leu Scee Kung (Port)

It was rumored that in a small village in Leu Scee Kung, in the Thirteenth District in Sichuan, there were many illegal opium users. I was sent to there to inspect that village. Transportation was not convenient as there was no public transportation of any kind, and one had to either walk or take a bicycle. Since I wanted to be mobile and quick, I opted for the bicycle. I also took along with me five armed assistants. At 2:00 p.m., we started out and arrived there at 5:00 p.m. The place was, in fact, hardly bigger than a hamlet of four or five families, a far cry from being a village. There were only four men, and two women addicts; we questioned, examined, and "booked" them. I had wanted to return that very evening, but it was already getting dark and beginning to drizzle, so we decided to wait till the next morning. As it is, traveling was very inconvenient, plus we had an additional six "addict-offense persons" traveling with us. If anything were to happen to them, our responsibilities would be too great.

Next morning it felt very cold; looking out, the roofs were covered with a heavy frost. Fortunately, we had stayed overnight. When everyone was ready, we set off. Mr. Wu, one of my assistants, led the way while I brought up the rear and marched forward. We walked along the paths and small roads, which traversed the field toward the actual village. As we neared the village center, we started to walk along a small stream, which may be the irrigation ditch between fields. On the way, there were many mounds and dips with frozen water in them. I was riding the bicycle, which suddenly slipped on some ice, and I fell into the ditch. Fortunately, the water was not too deep, but I did get thoroughly wet like a drowned chicken. My assistance dragged me out of the water. My coat and pants were soaked, but luckily, my upper body was not too wet as I was well protected by my thick woolen coat. We were taken to the "head" of the local government office and met Mr. Po, who immediately came and started to take everything off me, afraid that I might catch a cold. He apologized to me the entire time, saying, "This is all my fault, so sorry, so sorry. *Dwe bu chi* ['cannot face you,' or excuse me)."

"It is not your fault. Please, don't apologize," I said.

That night he said he had prepared a special banquet to appease my difficulties, but somehow it never came about. This Mr. Po, about sixty years old, was a typical old-fashioned civil servant and somewhat of a 'village elder.' He fussed around me for a long time, afraid that I would get ill. I thanked him and told him to put those illegal opium-addict persons in jail without further ado. When they were settled in jail, my assistants and I were glad to head back for home.

Er (Second) Jia Tsen—Opium Detox Association

My next assignment was to go to the Er Jia Tsen in the Ninth District of Nantung. It was at the midpoint between Shieng Cheng and Leu Scee Kung, where I had just left. When we arrived, the district head, Mr. Lee, also a civil servant, and the local chapter of the Opium Detox Association were organizing a meeting to educate the people about the evils of opium and how to stop the habit. They had erected a platform, which was a table acquired from the café in front of which the meeting was taking place. Mr. Lee saw me and immediately asked me to get up on the "platform." Many people had gathered in front of the café, and as soon as I got up on the table, they started to boo and shout. A certain Mr. Cheu even asked me to step down, but I did not pay any attention to him and instead stared down at the people making the most noise. Mr. Lee waved one arm and shouted above the din, "Quiet, quiet," and wiped his brow with his other arm because he was nervous and was sweating profusely.

"Don't worry," I said quiet softly. Suddenly, there was dead silence. I quickly used this opportunity and began to speak before the ruckus returned.

"I am only one person from outside your district, and I have been here only a very short time, and I am not familiar with your local customs, so really, I should not be standing here speaking to you all. However, I do work in the headquarters of the Smoking Cessation Office in Nantung, and it seems to me you are having a 'smoking cessation' meeting. Your supervisor, Mr. Lee, had asked me to come and say a few words. Honestly, I have no right to say anything, but because of Mr. Lee's kindness, I am inappropriately here. With no further consideration, I will step down." So saying, I started to climb down from the table. A few students ran toward me and held my legs, shouting, "Comrade, committee member, please, continue. We welcome you." (I later learned that they called everyone comrade.) Then many people intoned, "Welcome, welcome, welcome. Speech, speech."

How to begin? I pondered. Then I said, "I remembered that sentence spoken by Lin TseHsu during the Ching dynasty:

'If we smoked ten years, no one will be able to pay taxes.

In one hundred years, no one can fight our wars.'

Then I tried to explain these few words to the people. I spoke about the effects of opium with no holds barred, and tears up in my eyes. The sound of clapping and cheers were loud when I finished and as I came down from the platform. Many people rushed up to me to shake my hands. I shook hands with Mr. Lee who was also very moved and said,

"Hope there are more earnest people like you."

Then my friend Tsan Juen who had come with me from Nantung said, "KeSha, so you are an orator. Ordinarily, you seem to be so quiet and humble while, in fact, you are one of those modest people who hide their capabilities. Sorry, so sorry I misunderstood and underestimated you."

I was going to say, "Heart speak, straight speak'; but Mr. Lee interrupted, "I consider that what your comrade just said is from his heart and guts. Not only did he move me to tears, but I also saw several stubborn troublemakers wipe away tears from their faces. Brother, I do not like to flatter people, but I think you are not only an orator, but it is your sincerity that moved people."

"I thank you for your compliments," I replied.

"Please, prepare the Second Smoking Cessation Association for our district," said Mr. Lee. Thus, I was sent to the Ninth District in Nantung of the Smoking Cessation Association Office to open another branch.

I was now head of the Smoking Cessation Department in the Ninth District of Nantung. Near the main office was the district office's ancestral hall, which I think belonged to the Lee family because in the middle of the hall were many plaques of the Lee family going back several generations. At the end of this hall was a stage, and to the left, there was a *hwa ting* (flower hall), which we had converted into our office and our common room. I was assigned an assistant called Mr. Chang, who happened to live in this "all purpose" office. Near the hall was a large courtyard flanked by numerous cells, which could house over one hundred opium patients. The armed local police, who were supposed to protect this department, occupied the third side of the courtyard. Several male janitors were also sent to us to keep the place clean and hygienic. I worked here for half a year. We had had some success.

One evening, the leader of the Protective Police came to me and said, "These armed men will have to leave now."

"Then who will succeed them and protect us?" I asked.

"Oh, no one can. There is no one to take over. We received a secret order that we must go to the border shore area on the Yangtze River to protect the shores."

The war was now at our doorstep, so I did not inquire any further. Many opium smokers asked, "What has happened?" I did not think it was necessary to hide anything from them, so I told them, "Our country has received very heavy and tragic casualties because of the war. The Japanese have already surrounded Shanghai and Dachang and have sent soldiers along the north shore of Changjiang [Yangtse], so we need to send every available armed soldier to keep the Japanese from crossing the river."

At once, some asked worriedly, "Does this mean we will be kept here till we die?"

I said, "Don't worry, this is not your concern. The government will have solutions, I'm sure. You all belong here, and just by going out of these gates, you will be home. As for me, my home is tens of thousands of li away, and even if I wanted to go home, I cannot. Today, if the Japs come to attack, we cannot simply let them do so at will. We must fight back. I must now take leave from all of you. Early tomorrow morning, I am going to return to Hsiencheng and prepare to join the battle to drive the Japs back. You all take care. Remember try to resist that demon opium so that you can fight the Japanese."

As soon as I finished, several people came forward and surrounded me—some holding hands, some hugging my waist—but this frightened several of the armed guards and thought that the addicts would not let me go. They raised their guns and told them to leave me alone. Suddenly, one man, weeping, shouted, "Comrade, comrade, you must take care of yourself. Even though we are uneducated, we understand you more than you think we do. Ever since you came here, you had taken care of us night and day and gave us such earnest and careful instructions that we are determined to quit smoking. Our motherland is being attacked by the Japanese, and if we do not correct ourselves properly, we cannot even be compared to the dogs and pigs."

I thought this man's words were not like any of the others, so I looked at him closely again and discovered that he was the man who had asked me if they would be kept in the jail till death. I took his hands in mine and saw tears flow from his eyes; my own tears were also flowing fast. As this moment, Chang Lee brought the district leader toward me and said that he had just received a telephone call from HQ that the Number Two Smoke Cessation Association should be closed and that I should immediately return to Hsien Cheng. We returned to the office, and he again told me, "The Third Department also telephoned to say that conditions are very sensitive and that everything, personal and official, must be moved to the countryside to avoid being bombed. Only I will remain in Hsien Cheng. You must go to the Liu DoQuen's regoment to help him."

Liu DoeQuen did not have the demeanor of a soldier; he was artistic and a very gentle man. During the day, he and I went to the countryside to 'break' advancement, i.e., dig trenches and build 'hides' and other obstacles against the Japanese. At night, I recorded everything while he went to his *fen leu o* to 'play.' One day he said to me that he had written several pairs of door-side plaques and asked whether I had any good poems for him to write. I was surprised and casually asked him, "How about Li HouTsu's Ling Tao Ssa poem?" He was very happy.

I then asked him, "To whom will you present it?"

He blushed and replied that he was going to give it to a lady friend. I asked him whether he intended to marry her. "Now that is a very difficult question, and ordinarily, it would not be so difficult. But now I am in Nantung, and my home is north of Yaoyen. On top of that, I am now a soldier, moving and living here and there, with no fixed abode. How can I ask her to marry me? Think about it." He looked sad and crestfallen.

Then I said, "In this case, this pair of lines is not particularly suitable."

He replied, "It is perfectly suitable to both our circumstances."

I explained, "When Li HouTsu wrote this poem, he had been under house arrest and had lived a tragic and regretful life, even though that was not entirely like our present circumstances. His freedom had been curtailed by his enemy. Your lady friend cannot love the person she really wants but must laugh and entertain people for whom she does not care. How sad." I remembered a sentence by Bei ChuYi:

"We are all people sent to the border areas to suffer and weep."

I sighed as thoughts of Mma, Baba, my sister and Bei-Yuin, my white horse and the little horse boy who loved him so much, crowded into my head and I wondered where Mr. Koo, my English teacher, was and if he had managed to return to England before this dreadful war broke out, or if my father's loyal batman was safely and happily established in his small farm in Dawu, or our servant girl whom I used to chase around our back garden—all these thoughts cascaded through my brain and body like those rapidly flowing rivers 'at home.'

Then my assistant sighed and said, "Come, come, let us go for a drink and forget our depression and the war for a little while."

I said, "Let me finish my report, and then we can go for a drink." From then on, we became very sympathetic friends. Several times he came to look for me, but I was never home. Finally, he left me a note, saying that he had been transferred away from Nantung.

"Later," he wrote, "our future meetings may take place when things will be extremely dangerous—like high waves. I do not have many words, but my feelings are long and profound. We may not meet again."

Man's life is so short, but his sufferings are ever long.

This must be the nature of human life.

Chapter 5

CHOWHSU AND FAMILY, MARRIAGE

There were even fewer things to do when we moved the offices to the countryside. Except for a few old office mates, all the other employees came from elsewhere. We were only in the office when we only had something to do; otherwise, the rest of the time we spent together in one another's rooms, chatting, reading, or else running for the bomb shelter when we heard the alarm sirens. At night, we had to take turns to walk around the compound, but none of us stayed out too long. We were between the autumn and winter seasons, so the weather was becoming colder and colder.

During these colder months, MC contracted a respiratory illness and had to be hospitalized. I went to visit him one day and met a lovely nurse called ChowHsu, who was attending to him. MC introduced me to her.

"Miss Chow, meet Hsueh ChiPei, my childhood friend from Khangding."

I had never been formally introduced to a young lady before and blushed. My normally quick wit left me speechless. MC eyed me with suspicion.

"Ah, look at him. He who is usually so quick with his words is now dumb as a donkey in front of a pretty girl."

I blushed even more, mumbled something, and left. However, over the days MC was in the hospital, ChowHsu and I became better acquainted, and my awkwardness diminished. When the weather got even colder, she surprised me by giving me a thick wool sweater she had knitted. The other fellows in my office were very envious and persuaded me to ask ChowHsu to knit them one too. She did and gave one to Mr. Wong and Mr. Kuang who were ecstatic. ChowHsu was a beautiful woman from Yangchow, about two years younger than me. She worked in the nearby hospital and was one of the nurses who helped with the 'addict patients.'

She was kind but very tough with them. They all were very fond of her but also feared her because she did not spare her words if she discovered that they secretly had a puff or two. We had much in common, including our common friendship with Wang MungChow and Chinese opera, and we spent many a happy hour with each other, singing verses from one or the other operas. Another thing we had in common was that we loved to eat crabs. Almost every Sunday, when we had the chance, we would cycle to the countryside and find our favorite little café and order crabs. One day we arrived during the midmorning and ordered some freshly caught and steamed crabs and sat down to eat them. There was so much to talk about, that we completely forgot the time and amount we were eating. The shells began to pile up in front of us until we had to look around the huge pile to talk to each other. Finally, the proprietor of the little establishment came out and said to ChowHsu, "*Xiaojieh* [young miss], you cannot eat any more crabs. You will get sick."

We looked at each other and at the huge mound of shells between us and laughed for a long time then said to the poor astonished man, "Yes, you are right. We should stop, but we should be heading back home anyway. Thank you for your kind concern."

The final cement in our relationship was our love for the Sung and Tang poetry. I would often start a stanza, which she would finish. We tried to find poems we could not finish for each other, but we could not.

She had two younger sisters and two brothers. The older of the brothers, ChowTong, was already in the army and rising fast through the ranks. The older of the two sisters had just graduated from BeiDa University in Beijing with a degree in physics and was doing research in radiology. The two younger ones were still in middle and primary school. Her mother came from the family of a rich businessman. Like most of the women in those days, her mother was not schooled. Chow Taitai was known for her piety and beauty. She had wanted to enter a nunnery so had refused all suitors until Hsu's father came along—it was love at first sight for her. Despite my father-in-law's later philandering, Chow Taitai loved and was faithful to her husband till the very end. As evidence of her upper-class background, she also had bound feet. Unlike her mother, ChowHsu herself was educated, mostly due to a very forward-thinking and patriarchal grandfather. When this long bearded and longhaired old patriarch heard that the women in the house had started to bind his first granddaughter's feet, he rushed into the women's quarters, shouting all the way, "Stop! Stop that foot-binding at once. That was a rule set by a mad and selfish emperor. How dare you women torture and deform my granddaughter?"

He then took the terrified and crying Hsu in his arms and comforted her, saying, "Don't cry now. Ye-Ye [Grandpa] is here." Then he personally cut off the seven yards of binding cloth from each of her feet, which were already being tortured into their unnatural chicken-feet form. The women of the family shook their heads and murmured under their breaths, "No man will ever consent to marry a woman with large peasant's feet."

Hsu's feet were never bound. Furthermore, Hsu's grandfather insisted that she be sent to school with her younger brother, an almost unheard-of thing. Not only did she excel, but she was also top of her class and always beat her brother in everything except sports. Hsu finished her high school and became a trained midwife and a nurse. Fortunately, for her, she inherited the strong and fearless temperament from her adored grandfather.

Good-bye to Nantung and the Yang Chow Countryside

One day Hsu came to tell me that she had got permission from the hospital supervisor for a few days' leave to return to Yangchow to visit her mother and sisters and brothers. The principal, Yuen Tsang, of the hospital where Hsu worked asked her to take his daughter back to Taichow, which was not too far from Yangchow. I thought about the situation. Nantung was already a dangerous place while Yangchow was still relatively safe from the Japs. I thought it was a good idea, and I encouraged her to go and visit her family while there was still a chance. Then I thought about it further. I could not bear the thought of her being away for those many days, and with the way conditions were, one could never tell if she would be able to return to Nantung. So, I decided to accompany her and help her take Principal Yuen Tsang's daughter with us. There was a bus between Nantung and Taichow three times a day every other day, but we decided not to wait for a day and go by rickshaw. At 6:00

a.m. the next day, we hired three rickshaws and started our journey. We arrived shortly after 3:00 p.m. at Taichow and the girl's house. We handed her over to her mother, who was very happy to see her. She invited us to stay and have some tea and *tieng-xing* (snacks), but we thanked her, saying that we still had a long way to go to get to Yangchow; then immediately, we were on our way. I asked the head rickshaw puller, "Will we reach Yangchow today?"

He replied, "This is normally a two-day journey if we are not rushed, but if you want us to, we can get there in the middle of the night, but you will still have to pay us for two days." We discussed for a short while, and he continued, "But if we were to arrive by seven or eight, you will have to pay extra." We agreed. The rickshaw pullers were happy and said, "We will go as fast as we can."

At 6:00 p.m., we arrived. So in addition to the two-day fee, we gave each of them an extra tip of 1.5 yuan. They were exceedingly happy and contended.

"You are indeed generous and will become a high official one day and have many children." We thanked them for being so quick and wished them a safe return journey.

Hsu's mother, Chow Bei-Mu, was living with her Second, ChowPo, and Third daughter (ChowChi) and a small brother (ChowFu). ChowPo had returned from Beijing to be with her family during the war. They lived in town on Xiao Bei Street, two doors from their uncle. When Chow Bei-Mu saw Hsu, she rushed as fast as she could on her small bound feet to hug her eldest daughter. Crying, she said, "Aya, my shin-gan [*heart-liver,* Chinese words of endearment], you have come back?" and she would not let go of her.

"I got leave from the principal to come and visit Mother and sisters and little brother," Hsu replied, trying to calm her mother down.

"Everything is very dangerous now. What shall we do? Where shall we go?"

"We must all go the countryside. San Li-an is only about twenty li from Yangchow, and we still have old friends there. Tomorrow, you take sister and brother and go. I will remain in town with my friend now and take care of the house." Then Hsu introduced me to her family as the children were eyeing me with great curiosity.

"This is Hsueh ChiPei, my colleague at the Smoking Cessation Detox Center."

The family looked at me peculiarly as if I were foreigner because I was taller than anyone there, I had very curly hair, and my double-lidded eyes were larger than usual.

Hsu smiled and said, "He is from Sikhang and grew up among the Tibetans, but he is not a foreigner. He is Han (Chinese)." Everyone breathed a sigh of relief.

But Chow Bei-Mu would not hear of leaving her eldest daughter behind and insisted Hsu go with us while she herself stayed. So, it was decided we would all leave the very next day without Chow Bei-Mu. Hsu was very unhappy, but she was needed to take care of everybody and everything.

Escape to San LiAn BiLau

On the way from Yangchow, we stopped in a small village called San LiAn, which was north of Yangchow, and approached by the north gate of the town. Hsu wanted to take her small brother and two younger sisters and her cousin brother with us. About four *li* (slightly shorter than an English mile) from San LiAn, we decided to break our journey with Number One Uncle's good friend Bei LaoDi. Unfortunately, Uncle Bei's house was too small to accommodate all six of us, so we were taken to his son's place. Bei LaoDi's granddaughter used to work as a servant girl in the Chows' family home. However, Bei LaoDi's daughter-in-law was not at all happy with the situation and complained that there were too many of us and there would be too much confusion in the entire household, but she had no choice and had to let us stay because the Bei family was very close to the Chow family. The wife squeezed all six of us into one small room with only two beds. We had to share the kitchen, which we could not enter and use until they had finished their meal. Of course, we had no choice either and had to accept what we were given. Less than a week later, we heard that the Japanese had occupied Yangchow. Hsu cried bitterly and begged Bei LaoDi—who, though employed by Hsu's father, was like a real uncle to her—to go and fetch her mother. Bei Lao sent his son because he was afraid that if he were caught, he might be forced to be a 'coolie' (common laborer) or worse, a soldier for the Japanese Army. Then Bei LaoDi comforted Hsu and said, "Your mama is a very religious and helpful Buddhist, and most Japanese are Buddhists. I am sure no harm will come to her. Child, I am your father's friend through thick and thin. You are like my own daughter. I will help you in any way you want me to."

Suddenly, his daughter-in-law rushed into the room and said, "Quickly, hide. The devil has come to investigate."

"Quick, hide. The 'short devils' are in town." We were all worried and scared. We looked around and did not see anywhere to hide. Then Bei LaoDi's son said, "The gap, the gap between the two walls."

Most farmhouses in that district had two walls with ten to twelve inches of space in between them. This gap was normally used as a storage place for dried goods. It was very narrow, with just enough space for one person standing side by side the length of the wall. We all squeezed into the gap and held our breaths.

After about half an hour, which seemed like days, Bei LaoDi said, "Okay, everything is okay. Nothing will happen." He continued, "An armed 'devil', accompanied by a traitor, came to post a notice on our village wall, which said that 'nothing would happen to this village.'

Relieved, we squeezed out of our fine hiding place.

At once, Hsu's cousin brother and I went to the village to read the notice on the wall. There was a large crowd there already. Some were reading, and some were confused and worried because many could neither read nor write. We pushed ourselves to the front and read out aloud for everyone to hear, 'The Japanese Army has arrived here. We are here to help China fight against and destroy their enemy, the Communists.'

I have always remembered this. Japan already considered itself the conquering nation, and we were the conquered and had to obey. The Communists were, after all, Chinese. I was furious; all I wanted to do was tear down the notice. Hsu's cousin held me and said, "You cannot do this. We must tolerate, and we must wait and see how long they can continue their evil ways."

Lao TaiTai's Home—SaGo

About a week later, Bei LaoDi and his son brought Chow Lao TaiTai to the countryside to join us. With them, they also brought a cousin sister who was a cripple. Chow Bei-Mu knew that Bei LaoDi was not rich, and to feed and accommodate these additional seven or eight people will certainly breed problems, so she decided that our family should all go to her *lao-jia* (old family home) in SaGo. Bei LaoDi saw the virtue in this and agreed but still protested, "Aya, Chow Taitai, your family has been so good to us, and yet we cannot repay you in these urgent times when you most need us. I am so sorry."

"Bei LaoDi," said Chow Bei-Mu, "don't worry yourself so. It is impossible for all of us stay with you. You have already risked your life in coming to Yangchow to fetch us. All those Japanese, swarming about the town, were terrifying to my children and me. Without you and your son, how could we even be here? So don't worry yourself. Just help us get to SaGo."

Because it was a town by the sea, most of the people in SaGo were fishermen, so they traveled around by boats. We had to pass Lu YangHu, which was a lake between Yangchow and Tangcheng, on the way to SaGo. The other enterprise of this area was the transportation of night soil collected from the villagers' outhouses via long low boats. The night soils were gathered in large wooden buckets and put in the lower level of these boats and then shipped and sold to neighboring farmers as fertilizers. It was a thriving business, but only few people were willing to do this rather smelly job. When we arrived at the lake, these were the only boats available for hire. Most of the other "normal" passenger boats were either hidden or destroyed to avoid being commandeered by the Japanese.

Usually, the night-soil boats had two levels: the household and helpers lived in the upper level while the night soil was contained in buckets in the lower lever. Fortunately, for us, the night-soil boat we had rented carried no night soil, and it was in such a boat that we hid to escape being checked enroute as the smell was suffocating and a strong deterrent against the Japanese guards. They never checked them.

Bei LaoDi's son realized that it was not comfortable in the boat and that we would be missing the beautiful countryside of Yangchow we were passing; and every time, when he was sure that there were no Japanese soldiers or any 'traitors' lurking on the banks, he would ask us upstairs to get some fresh air and enjoy the scenery. We were approaching the beautiful YuLan Lake. It was winter already, and ahead, we saw the willow branches with yellowing leaves swaying gently in the breeze. The long 'weeping' branches were almost glancing the surface of the calm lake. There were people on the banks of the lake, and we were afraid and did not know whether to stay above or sneak down below. Bei LaoDi's son smiled and said, "We have arrived. We are in SaGo."

Hsu held Lao TaiTai while I looked after the little ones. We got off the boat and stepped onto the dock. The 'stone has fallen on the ground' as the saying goes, and our hearts were relieved.

SaGo was not a large town. It was, in fact, quite a small but lively place; and very quickly, we arrived in Chow BeiMu's home. We were greeted by a middle-aged lady, who, when she realized who the Lao TaiTai was, quickened her pace and approached her and hugged her, tears flowing freely.

"Second Sister, ah, Second Sister, you really worried us. At last, you have returned home." Then pointing to me, she continued, "I know you and your sisters and brothers, but who is this young man?"

Lao TaiTai put her mouth to her ears and whispered something. She beamed and said "Hao, hao, hao" over and over. We were all made to refresh ourselves and then on to dinner. After the meal, Bei LaoDi's son said that he had many friends in SaGo and would stay in Li-An tonight and return tomorrow instead. He then took my shoulders and said, "You are alone and a stranger from far away, and yet you accompanied ChowHsu to Yangchow, then helped her and her family to move to SaGo. I do admire your initiative and bravery."

I said, "Bei DaGe, please, don't mention it. Don't be so generous in your praises. Later, when there is an opportunity, I will come to see you and your father, Bei LaoDi."

Alas, more than half my life is over, I have not seen him again, and I never did learn his real given name, only as Bei *DaGe* (Bei elder brother).

That night Yima, Chow BeiMu's sister, lit a pair of big red candles and said to me, "I am sending you to a neighbor of mine, to an old lady's house to stay, because I do not have room here."

Hsu and I followed her to the neighbor and saw a white-haired old grandma with Buddhist rosary beads in one hand and mumbling something. Yima pointed to Hsu and said to me, "Tonight is your wedding night. You two will be traveling far and wide, so because of convenience, I am marrying Hsu to you. It will be easier for you to travel together in the future. Now we are escaping from the Japanese, everything must be simplified." She wept, handed Hsu over to me, and said, "Child, you must take care of her well."

I was dumbfounded but immediately agreed. I followed Yima with the very large red candle into a very small room with one bed and one desk. Yima put the candle down and continued, "You should rest now. You have been very busy the whole day."

The white-haired Lao TaiTai chuckled and said, "You must know that this is a very fertile bed." Hsu was so overwhelmed that she could not even lift up her head. This must be the simplest and quickest wedding in the history of China!

The Family of Hsu's Mother in SaGo

Later, Lao TaiTai took Hsu and me as she wanted to take me to 'show me off, the new son-in-law,' to her own cousin sister, the daughter of her mother's sister. They also lived in SaGo, and when they were growing up together, they were like 'blood sisters.' When they approached the house, Lao TaiTai's cousin saw us and ran to embrace us. "Second Sister, Second Sister," tears running down both their cheeks.

Then she took Hsu's hands and said, "I hear you are very busy and doing very well. You are a very good daughter." Then looking up, she said, "This must be our new cousin brother, *Sing GuYe*." (New brother-in-law).

I quickly answered, "You are too kind to call me that, BeiMu. Please call me ChiPei." Then I gave a deep bow, much to everyone's amusement.

BeiGu said, "I am relieved that you all got out peacefully. Please rest here for a few days and see how the situation develops. The Japanese devils oppressed us Chinese and have been barbaric. I'm afraid the war will not be a short one this time. You young people must look clearly and act well. Later, China's future lies in your hands."

I heard these words and realized the truth and importance of them. They were like seeds sown in the ground, making only quiet whispering sounds or none.

Hsu had told me that her SaGo Bei GuMa was an unusual and beautiful woman. She was both very capable and understood the political situation, which was very advanced for a woman in those times. She also performed heroic deeds like running an entire household despite her totally dissipated husband.

Lao TaiTai (as Hsu's mother was known, though she was far from old) said,

"That family was a rather high clan, who were not only beautiful and generous but were also highly educated and very cultured. Unfortunately, the cousin's husband was not the same. He eventually contracted the 'pleasure house disease' (syphilis) and was never allowed to share his wife's room, though he continued to live in the house till his end. The entire household's duties were carried out and supervised by Lao TaiTai's cousin. The older generation trusted her, and the younger generation respected her so much that they considered her like a goddess. Even her dissipated husband, when he needed some petty cash, must kowtow to her. When we were taken to see her, she was very happy and asked us to stay with her for a few days. She accompanied us every day and said that when the war is over and there is peace, we must go and live with her. Later, when the Communists arrived in SaGo, they had to flee to Shanghai, after which we lost touch with that family and never saw them again. When I was in Anhwei, we received news that they were safe; but after, there was no more news, and we never saw them again. She had had such a difficult and tragic life, but she made the most of it. Whenever I thought of her, I blamed heaven for being so unfair.

Yao Family in Yiencheng

Lao TaiTai told me that the Yao family in Yiencheng was Hsu's father's 'blood' brother and that we should go and visit him too. He may have some news of Hsu's father. Lao TaiTai asked her elder sister to take care of her three younger children then took Hsu and me to visit Yao BeiBei. Yiencheng was in the district of Jiangsu near the sea. The Yao family lived in the town and was of some renown. As soon as Yao TsungBei saw us, he called out, "Congratulations, congratulations, you have peacefully returned. You had me terribly worried, Little Sister." Then turning to Hsu, he said, "Is this the young man who had written a letter to us addressed to Small White Street, eh? It should have been called White Small Street."

I had misaddressed it. That was why Hsu had not received my letter. So, when I sent another, I had written on the back of the envelope; but before I could say another word, Yao BeiBei said, "Ah, it is something you had written on the back of the envelope that impressed me: 'If there is no Xiao BeiJe, then please send it to Bei XiaoJe.'"

We all had a good laugh at that. Hsu then asked her uncle whether there was any news of her father. "Many months, no news," Yao BeiBei replied regretfully. "I have read from the newspapers that his regiment is in He-Nan. Other than that, nothing. But let us not talk of those matters since you have just arrived. You must stay a while."

Then he told the servants to prepare the two outside rooms. Hsu and Lao TaiTai stayed in the large guest room while I stayed in the small study, where they put up a small bed. It was not easy staying with the Yao family as I felt that we were imposing on them. It was very awkward. Yao BeiBei told me that there was a small school nearby that needed a teacher and asked if I would like to apply for the job. I told him that I wanted to take Hsu to her father.

"I will consider the teaching job later when we have met Uncle Chow," I said to Yao BeiBei, who was disappointed.

That night Yao's children said to me, "You living in our house, separated from your new bride, is not right. Are you giving her the cold shoulder?"

I then realized that they wanted me to go, so I said, "I am not cold to her. This is her father's friend's house, not her own house, so things are awkward. But rest assured, we will repay you later."

I discussed the situation with Hsu and BeiGuMa, who said that we must immediately move into her house. Just to get a reaction, we told Yao BeiBei that we wanted to visit BeiGuMa for a while. He agreed in one breath. So, we moved into BeiGuMa's house. She was afraid that we would get bored, so she often had friends and neighbors over to dine and play mahjong, though we ourselves did not know how to play.

One day Bei GuFu came to ask me, "Do you know that your father-in-law is the Seventy-first Regiment's commander?"

I was surprised and asked, "How do you know? Where did you get this information?"

"They are all talking about it in the streets. There was some sort of meeting in my school."

"Then where is he?" He could not answer, so I went to ask Yao BeiBei, who said, "I also heard this news and that he is in Henan, Loyang." I had to go to Yao Bei-mu to get the exact address because I had wanted to go there immediately. We got the answer very fast. As a matter of fact, Seventy-first Regiment was in MieNorr near Shanxi. I remember the name MieNorr because of the two-thousand-year-old story about the "return" of the carved *yu* (jade) called NingXiang Yu back to Emperor Tsao. Now two thousand years later, we are still talking about this story. I asked Yao BeiBei to send a telegram to Hsu's father.

"Hao, hao [all right], I'll try," he said. Amazingly, the telegram was sent; and shortly thereafter, we received a reply, telling us that we should wait for him in Loyang. Hsu was very happy and excited with the news, but she wanted to go to Loyang immediately, saying that she would first return to SaGo herself to LaoTaiTai while I can stay on in Loyang. When things settle down, then we will return to Yangchow together. Hsu and I took the quick steamboat from Yiencheng to Lunyun and then to Suchow. From there, we took the train to Zhengshiang and changed train to Loyang. When we arrived in the Suchow station, it was already 4:00 p.m. We found that there were no trains to Zhengchow till 1:00 or 2:00 a.m. I found a hotel room nearby to rest for a few hours. It was a small room with a single bed but had a mosquito net. It was only 4:00 p.m., but the room was already dark and lit by a tiny little light. I heard the mosquitoes buzzing around us. Hsu was afraid of mosquitoes, so I told her to get under the net. After a while, I joined her under the net too. Very soon, we fell into a deep sleep. We had been traveling hard and far and had not realized how extremely tired we were. Alas, not long after, I felt my body itching unbearably, and I quickly rose to see what had happened. The bedbugs were having a feast. I awakened Hsu.

"What's the matter?" she asked, irritable.

"Bedbugs—hundreds, thousands of them!" I exclaimed.

"Where are they?" I pointed to a row of them to her. She was surprised as there was not even one on her side of the bed and not a single bite on her. With one stroke of my arms, I left a line of my blood. I saw the bedbugs had crawled up to the top of the mosquito net. I could no longer sleep. It was odd. Mosquitoes plagued Hsu but not the bedbugs, while I, on the other hand, was attacked by both beasts. We gave up the room and were glad to escape the bedbug/mosquito palace.

At 1:00 a.m., we arrived at the train station but had to wait a while longer. It was difficult to tell if the train would come or had already left. Things were so uncertain. During those times, the locomotives of the trains were painted either in green or in blue to denote "special usage." This was used by the BeiTsun Kuang to go to the front line. We did not mind which commander was using the train. We just wanted to get on one. We paid a porter one yuan to put our luggage on the train. He was very pleased. In the train, I saw a vendor selling edibles. He started to tout his ware, "This is the famous roast chicken" or "This is the famous Suchow onion pancakes," and so on.

We had not eaten anything since that morning, and we did not mind whether it was famous, so we bought a chicken and two onion cakes. These were the most delicious *dien-xin* we had eaten for a long time. The train whistle sounded, and we chugged out of the station.

Chiangsu District—Tseng Show JingPao (Escape from the Japanese)

We sat on a bench in the station, waiting for the train for Luoyang, when suddenly the *jingpao* sounded. Air raid—telling us to run, hide, go to a shelter, etc. The Japanese were here. We dragged our luggage and ran toward the empty space away from the station. We looked up and saw a plane aiming for the station. We threw ourselves on the ground; two sounds of loud bombings and a sequence of machine guns broke around us. Lying in front of me was a big man in a soldier's uniform, whose big bottom was in front of me; but when he heard the machine guns, he got up and tried to run. I slapped him hard on his rear and shouted over the din, "During the machine-gun fire, you must never move, or you will be discovered, and we will all be mowed down. You are a soldier. How could you forget such a basic rule in military training?"

He stammered, "Don't be angry. I was so nervous, so I moved thoughtlessly. Please forgive me. I could have got all of us killed."

I said, "Sorry, I criticized you just now. The Jap devils want to annihilate all of us. Such events will happen over and over. Don't forget."

Finally, the *jingpao* (alarm) stopped. He turned to me and saluted, "I will remember what you said just now. I came from Shanxi and was preparing to go to Wuchang for military training."

Then we parted, and Hsu and I went to the Luoyang station and caught the green train.

Chapter 6

GANYI AND RENTSE

Hsu's father was a man of steely determination, steadfast and resolute, *gan-yi* but also full of *ren-tse* (compassion) for his regiment and for people in general. But he was also not a man to be crossed without a good reason. Chow Bei Bei had been the chief of the Number Five Tsengchiang Police Station, but now he was with General Gu TsoTung in Wang Nawu, south of Anhwei, but we did not know exactly where he was.

We arrived at Luoyang station at 3:00 p.m. and hired a rickshaw to take us to the hotel recommended by Hsu's father in his telegram. As soon as we arrived, a uniformed officer, holding a baton, was waiting for us at the doorway of the hotel. He called out, "Chow Hsu." (I later discovered that his family addressed all their children by their surname, then given name together.) "You have arrived. Get in the car," he instructed.

As soon as we saw the car, Hsu cried out, "Baba." There was a private car parked at the hotel's driveway, and within it was a uniformed officer in the backseat. Father and daughter were united. After a few minutes, Hsu's father asked, "How are your mother, little brother, and your sisters? I am sorry I did not satisfy the fatherly responsibilities of protecting them. Now the country is in massive confusion. In trying to take care of the country, I have neglected my family." His voice sounded sad and tragic. Then he continued, "Get in the car. We will talk some more when we arrive at my camp. We still have some ways to go." A middle-aged man in the hotel, maybe the manager, came up to Hsu's father and spoke to him, "Chu Tsang [Department Head], please stay here a night. Let us take care of you, your daughter, and son-in-law. I want to give them a welcome party."

Father thanked him and apologized, "Thank you very much, but there is much to do, and we must leave at once."

Then turning to me, he said, "So, Chow Hsu, this your young man?" looking at me up and down. "He looks like a soldier." Then turning to me, he asked, "And what is your name, and where did you come from?"

"Hsueh ChiPei, Chow Chu Tsang," I replied.

He laughed out aloud, "Do not call me that. Call me Baba. After all, you are Hsu's husband." Hsu pulled at my sleeves and smiled embarrassedly. We were all followers of Confucius, and it was not considered 'manly' or good manners to show one's emotions.

I continued, "I come from Khanding, Sikhang."

"Oh. You are a very long way from home." Baba raised an eyebrow. "How did you get here? And where is your family?" He had many questions, and by and by, I told him on our way to his camp.

"You poor boy, you have left all your loved ones behind, and all your friends are elsewhere because of this war. I hope you get to see them again."

I did lose many of them, and most of them I never saw again. We headed for a remote town called Ming Tser near Shanxi. This town was famous from the times of the San Kuo (Three Kingdoms) around 600 BCE. We were now in the Henan District near the border of Shanxi—a very desolate place of *huang tu* (yellow sticky earth), a heavy clayey soil. It was not easy to dig; but once dug, the earth did not collapse, so it was good for bomb shelters. Most of the military offices were in these clayey caves, and they did not have to worry because they were safe from the bombings. The caves were swept and kept very clean, and they were very cool in the summer and strangely warm in the winter.

Outside the town, there was a river called YiLi He, which dated back to the Ming dynasty. Though it was not very deep, it was very clear, and one could see the bottom of the riverbed. The ladies used to form long chains along the banks and wash their clothing in the clear waters. It was very peaceful and quiet along the river; and in the middle, there were many fishing rods stuck in the bed, waiting for fish to bite. This was the main source of food for the local people.

Hsu's father lived in a small cave beside his "office cave," and there was really no room for all of us. Since there were no more caves dug, we had to rent a room in town about half a li from ChowBaba's office. This room was beside the landlord's room with a small grassy area in between, and during the harvest, wheat was winnowed on this space. Hsu looked on and commented, 'Very convenient.' Her father breakfasted with us before he went to his office. In the afternoon, he returned for dinner— yes, all very convenient. At first, the landlord wanted five yuan a month; but later, he wanted to increase his rent because he said he would ask his daughter-in-law to come and wash our clothes and help in the kitchen. We decided to give him ten yuan a month. Everyone was happy.

One day Hsu's father told Hsu to make a few more dishes as he had asked a few of his colleagues for dinner. Hsu asked the landlord if there was anywhere one could buy some pork and other things. He said, "Luckily, yes, this is market day, but you must go quickly, or the foodstuffs will be all sold out."

Hsu and I jumped up and wanted to run right away to the market, but Hsu's father laughed and said, "Slowly, don't rush. You are a lady now, no longer a child."

We took the landlord's daughter-in-law with us and walked to the market. We bought five *jing* pork, a big fish, one fat hen, some big and small prawns, fresh pears, broad beans, tofu, mushrooms, daikon radish, cabbage, and large amounts of scallion, garlic, and ginger. I was amazed and asked Hsu,

"So much meat and vegetables. Can you cook all this?"

 She replied, "I will try, and if I cannot do it, I must do it anyway. Baba has already invited several guests. I cannot let the old man down." We had plenty of time because it was only 10:00 a.m., so we had eight hours to get the feast on the table.

I joked, "If the guests were allowed to wait for two hours, then we will have ten hours—no problem!"

By then, Hsu and I had been together for nearly three years. I have never seen her enter the kitchen anywhere, let alone cook! When we were staying Bei LaoDi's daughter-in-law's house, she did go into the kitchen to make congee rice and noodles to fill our stomachs, but I never saw her make any real dishes or do any serious cooking. Somehow, she was not at all nervous. I thought that she might have some hidden talent. Hsu then asked the landlord if we could use his extra room since our own room was too small. (All Ming people had extra rooms to put their ancestors' plaques and other religious objects.) The landlord agreed immediately but requested that the leftovers be shared with them because they had never seen such a banquet being prepared. Hsu agreed; but in fact, even before the dishes were put on the table, she had already divided out a portion for the landlord and his family as she was afraid there would be no leftovers.

By 6:00 p.m., Hsu had prepared everything; and at 7:00 p.m., Chow Baba came with three guests. He introduced us to them: the first a bespectacled man named Mr. Du; the second a middle-aged man, Mr. Tsao; and the third, a younger man of about thirty, Mr. Chang. I saw that this Mr. Chang was wearing a single star on his collar; thus, he must be someone of note. Later, I learned that he was Lujuen Chiang Kuan's college mate but in a class higher. Hsu seated everyone then asked the landlord's daughter-in-law to bring in the dishes in order. There were four sets: fish, sautéed cabbage, peas, and fried prawns; second, a vegetable mix; third, *tun-po-rou*, a specialty pork dish of her mother's hometown; and, finally, *hong-sau* (red-cooked) fish.

Mr. Du exclaimed, "Da Xiao Jieh [Big Little Sister], your father had told me that you can cook. I had not believed him because young women of these days do not even go near the kitchen. I see my disbelief was totally wrong. Your father had also told me that your lion's head is even better. Did you make it today? Can you really make it?"

Hsu said, "Du Beibei, there was no minced pork today, so I made a Hongsau *dofu* instead." Hsu's father started to say something, but Mr. Du cut in and said, "You are lying. Is this *dong-po-rou* made of beef?"

Hsu did not say anything but returned to the kitchen with the landlord and came out with a large metal-covered dish. Hsu put the dish on the middle of the table and with a flourish removed the lid.

"Du BeiBei, this is the *hongsau dofu*."

Du BeiBei looked and loudly proclaimed, "You naughty girl, you dare to bluff your uncle Bei." Then he spoke to everyone, "This is lion's head. Color is good, aromatic. Taste must be good too. Come, let us eat." Then he took out two bottles of brandy (cognac) from his pocket and put them on the table.

Hsu's father asked incredulously, "Old Du, where did you get these valuables?"

Du said, "Sometime ago, some people came from Xian and presented a case of it to the army colonel who gave me two bottles. Luckily, I never had an occasion to use them till now. Today we will drink them with these delicious dishes."

"Du brother," said Mr. Tsao, "you are indeed a lucky man. No matter whatever difficulty you meet, with one slice of the knife's edge, you solve the problem."

Then Chang, who had been silent all this time, said, "You are all talking of this and that, but you all have forgotten one thing."

"What are you talking about? What one thing?" asked Mr. Du.

"You have forgotten that Chow Xiao Jieh has completed a great event. How could you forget that and not congratulate her?"

Du and Tsao were contrite. "Ah yes, we must be punished. We must be punished." Du then filled each person's wine cup, lifted his own, and faced Hsu's father, then turned to Hsu and me, and said, "I lift the offering up to eye level [for husbands], so hold your hands until hair turns white."

Hsu and I responded at once by saying, "Since leaving Nantung, this meal can be considered our first real 'wedding meal.' The food is good, wine is good, but also being with our father and his friends during times of war is very special and difficult. Let us enjoy being together. I cannot deny that heaven has given us such good fortune today."

That evening the whole family enjoyed the dishes Hsu made for us. Alas, our stomachs, not having had so much rich foods of late, could not digest them; and the next day we all had stomachaches and diarrhea. The landlord came and told Hsu that they do not want any more fish and meat because they very seldom eat these and their stomachs could not cope with such rich foods either; in any case, they will not be able to afford to buy such meats in the future. It is better not to develop a taste for such delicious dishes.

"However, we do not mind accepting leftover rice and vegetables," he finished his pronouncement.

Hsu told her father, who sighed and said, "Ever since the Japanese came to China, Henan has been plundered, and countless numbers of people were slaughtered, even though they were only crying from hunger and cold." He paused then continued, "Have you seen the little children climb the tall trees to pick seeds to eat?"

Hsu said that she had seen them and found it strange and wondered what they were doing. "Ah, so they were picking elm seeds to eat."

Hsu's father said that fortunately there were many here. Otherwise, the people would totally starve. After the meal, we all fell to pondering the war; the Communist Long March participants of Mao TseTung and Chiang KaiShek; and his 'scorched earth' strategies, in other words the general conditions of our poor country. Chow Baba and his friends arrived filled with good cheer but departed with bowed heads, shaking and sighing. Even Chow Baba who, I am told, almost never showed his worries looked tired and weary. To his soldiers, he always appeared cheerful and positive.

Riding Wild Horses

One day I saw quite a number of horses and riders begin to gather at a certain place; I knew all army regiments had their own horses and loved to ride them, but this was something special, so I asked Chow Baba,

"Is there going to be a horserace?"

"Yes," he said, "there will be a race and also a competition for the best rider."

Quite a few people had already gathered at the racecourse, but aside from the soldiers, there were also many peasants. A temporary platform had been erected, and the colonel was standing upon it. His friend, Ms. Wong, in a riding outfit, was standing to his right; and several high officials of the army were seated behind him. Mr. Chang and Mr. Tsao were the judges, and Chow Baba was the chief inspector. He was down among the horses and riders, inspecting the saddles, stirrups, bits, and the form and conditions of the competitors. He also came up onto the makeshift platform while Hsu and I squeezed among a large group of other spectators on the ground. Suddenly, a whistle sounded. Mr. Gao rode forward on a tall, large silver-gray European-bred horse. Ms. Wong descended from the platform, and the colonel's batman led a chestnut-brown spirited horse to her. The other competitors rode horses from Manchuria or Mongolia, and finally, there was one smallish horse of no great beauty, but he was very spirited and strong. This one was from the Ximing and Tisein Tsang area, I was certain.

Chow Baba said, "Now that is a wild and untamed horse. He often kicks and bites strangers."

I asked if I could try to ride him. Father refused, but then, Mr. Du asked me whether I knew how to ride.

I replied, "I grew up with horses. Riding is second nature to me. I could ride almost before I could walk. My father had over thirty horses in our stables."

Mr. Du said to Chow BaBa, "Let him ride. He grew up with horses. There should be no danger."

"All right, if you can mount him, you can participate in the races."

"I think this horse can run fast. I just wanted to test to see how fast he can really run. I am not interested in any prize."

Father then asked the mafu (horse tender) to lead the small horse over to me. I went over and patted his head and nose. He grunted and chewed his bit and nodded. I then patted him on the mane, and he tried to shy away, so I simply grabbed his mane and mounted him in one leap. He suddenly rose on his hind legs and whinnied and protested, but I held on to his mane with my left hand and with my right held the reins. I squeezed the stirrups with both my legs and feet. He stood still. Then I reached over and patted his neck. He calmed down and obeyed me at once. I cantered him over to the other horses. Mr. Du raised his thumb toward me, and both he and BaBa smiled. The horses were lined up neatly and stopped ten meters in front of the platform. Since I was the last participant to arrive, I was situated at the extreme outside of the line.

Tsun SeFe ordered, "Today's race: First run three times around the track. Then at the end of the fourth round, you must finish at the starting line. Get ready."

The gun fired, and the horses kicked up the dirt as they pounded off together. My "wild" horse lifted all four hooves off the ground as if his stomach was going to touch the ground. His tail stretched straight behind him like a taut rope, his ears pulled back. He was just like my Dragon King stallion. I felt as if my White Cloud had come back to me to let me ride in this race. I said quietly, "BeiYuin [White Cloud], you are with me." He was stable and utterly smooth. At the third round, he suddenly started to increase his speed. The front legs were like a bow and the hind ones like arrows, a single stride going many meters. We had not reached the midway point, but we had overtaken both Gao and Ms. Wong by 25 percent of the way. All the other horses were far away behind us. Of course, we came in first. Du BeiBei praised me, saying, "Wow, your ability to ride is so high. Have you been to the cavalry?"

"No, sir, I have not. But I grew up with horses. Sorry, I have not explained to you my circumstances, which is why you are so amazed at my riding prowess. Where I grew up, we all rode like this. I was born in Dawu in the Far Eastern region of Sichuan near Tibet. It was extremely remote and inaccessible, and except for horses and cows, we had no communication with the outside world. My father was the district commissioner and magistrate of the four neighboring districts and also the local governor and border controller of the Emperor. At home, we kept up to thirty horses, and ever since I can remember, I liked horses and had no fear of them. When I was six, I followed my father to Khanding on horseback. He had made a wooden seat and placed it on top of the saddle of my small horse, and the mafu led him by the reins. Many, many times, I pleaded with my father to let me ride rather than sit in the uncomfortable wooden seat, but my father would not. However, I used to ride without my father's knowledge. When he found out, he locked up the saddle, reins, and stirrups. This did not deter me. I simply grabbed the mane and jumped onto the horses and rode barebacked. I played 'soldiers and bandits' with the local boys, and we used to terrorize the villagers and had great times. The children there all learned how to ride like that, so I am not that unusual. It is the environment that shaped my riding skills."

Mr. Du was full of admiration and declared, "We should send you to the cavalry to 'show off' your talent, and yet you are so modest."

Later, Juen Tsang told me that I should be sent to the artillery school because he himself had graduated from the Huang Pu Military Academy.

Eventually, I went to the Su Tsan GanBu Training Academy. Chow Baba said that it was a good idea and that I should get ready to go right away.

"Go say good-bye to Hsu. You will see her again. Go to war college and get ready for our number one enemy."

That evening, I told Hsu what her father had told me and that I must leave tomorrow. It was not an easy parting as we were just getting used to being a married couple. Though we have been traveling together for about two years, it had been as colleagues and friends. Love was just beginning to surface, and now we must part. It was hard. Hsu was very understanding but did not say much. That night we held each other close, Hsu sobbing quietly beside me and I trying to be very Confucian! It was a night I will never forget or want to remember. At this age, such emotions tear the heart.

Chapter 7

THE NEW WARRIOR

After graduation, I was sent to the San Ming Ju Yi Propaganda Academy where I met Wu YienTse, who was the secretary of the HQ of the academy. I worked in the Education Department of the Kuo Ming Tang Party, and my main responsibility was to arrange for famous speakers for the academy. Two such people were Cheng LiFu and Yie JianYin, but our classrooms were small; and often we had to use the dining hall or the parade ground where we had to stand and listen. The last time Mr. Cheng spoke, he was so long-winded that we students composed a joke associated with him:

'We're not afraid of heaven, not of earth.

Just afraid of Cheng LiFu's dearth.'

Every time he lectured, it went on in a boring monotonous tone and would take four to five hours and many of us nodded off through his lectures.

Early one morning, our principal suddenly came unannounced to inspect our living quarters. We were very worried because the bathrooms had no water, so things were not spick-and-span. The assistant, ChengCheng, came to our dormitory and told us to bind the door handles to our bathrooms with wire, so they will not be opened. When everything was inspected, we were called to assemble in the hall. Fortunately, he was not really interested in the cleanliness of our dormitory. He had come to give us some important information.

The principal announced,

"The situation in Wuhan is dangerous, so we must dismantle and move to Tong Sa immediately." He encouraged us to keep up our spirits. "This is just when the country needs our protection." Many of us had not really seen combat. We were inexperienced and did not know what to expect. We returned to our dormitories at once to pack our belongings. I went to the library and removed two large dictionaries and put them into my pillowcases. I wanted to take them with me. My colleague Bei RenFu saw what I was doing and looked at me strangely and said,

"Are you mad? Those dictionaries are so heavy, and you are going to put them in your knapsack? Anyway, these kinds of dictionaries are updated frequently, so they will be out-of-date in a few years. Why do you want to carry them on your back?"

I replied, "During these times of continuous movement and confusion, I would not be able to find such dictionaries. These were from the Wuttang College library's special books, the 'treasures' section. We have stayed here for almost a year. We should be able to take some 'memory' with us. We cannot say what will be our future. At least we will have these treasures to remind us." I felt rather irritated, and my throat felt as if a "plum pit" had got stuck in it.

Bei LaoShen quickly said, "Sorry, I did not mean that you should not carry these dictionaries. I was concerned that they may be too heavy for you later," and he continued, "Okay, okay, if they are so precious to you, and when they become too heavy, I will help you carry them."

Wu YienTse came over and said, "Quickly, prepare your luggage. What are you two arguing about?" RenFu told YienTse what had happened.

YienTse said, "ChiPei, I admire your actions. RenFu's offer to help is a 'should be.'"

"But what about my wife? What will become of her?" I asked worriedly.

"She will be all right. She is now with her father, Chow Chu Tsang. They have left already. We will catch up to them. Let us get in the car, come on, we must depart."

Tsung principal, Dai TseQi, came to tell us to use ChengCheng, the assistant principal's name, and send a telegram to the station master to say that he must immediately attach carriages to the engine and be prepared to leave as soon as we all arrive. But the train did not arrive at the station till noon. YienTse, RenFu, Yao LiangGao, and I were together; and we hurriedly boarded the train and soon left Wuhan. Yao LiangGao, YienTse's secretary, was an honest and good fellow, but he loved his drink; and once drunk, he could eat a lot and become very fearful. YienTse, RunFu, and I spoke Sichuanese; but Yao was from Chiangsu/TsangYu, and we found his sing-song accent very funny. He did not act like a servant to YiehTse but rather treated him like an 'elder.' YienTse was going to BeiDa University to be a professor, but he never did make it because of the war.

Before the war, Yien Tse had gone to university in Japan where he lived with his wife for a few years. His professor had asked him to teach and lecture on the Chinese SceeTse poetry style and for which he received a small stipend. Time was hard in those times, so he accepted the job and held it till the end of his studies. Before he returned to Beijing, he had already been accepted into the BeiDa University. He had not imagined that Japan would be attacking China. He was furious when he discovered that BeiDa and the Japan University were affiliated, so he refused the position BeiDa had offered him. Instead, he joined the Sichuan's Li JaJow army, where he soon became the army secretary. He was much respected by all, and the soldiers called him Teacher Wu rather than Secretary Wu. He wanted to do more for his country, so he requested for a transfer to the Kang Training Academy. After graduation, he was sent to the San Ming JuYi Academy where we met, and now we were on our way to Chang Sha.

While we were chatting on the train, it stopped suddenly. We thought we had arrived at a small train crossing and had to let another train to pass, but we heard someone shout, "Enemy coming. Get off the train at once."

My three friends and I jumped off the train, and then we heard the enemy planes' automatic guns fire at the train. YienTse, not fearing for his life, ran toward a small bridge and jumped into the river, which, unfortunately, had no water. It was a dry riverbed. "Aya," he cried. I thought he was injured and also jumped down from the bridge and landed beside him. "Where are you hurt?" He pointed to his waist. I felt it and feared he had broken a rib, but aside from a large scratch on his skin, no other bones seemed to be broken. We had hardly finished speaking when we heard a loud bombing sound. The enemy had dropped a firebomb onto our train. It was not completely on fire. About ten minutes later, the enemy plane left. Slowly, we crawled out from under the bridge, inspected ourselves, and luckily no one was hurt. Dai Tseng commandant ordered the First Battalion to walk to Yueyang; from there, we could wait for another train to Changsha. My friends and I saw that the station was called Tsung HuoPu.

RenPu then came up to me, looking very contrite; he apologized and said that while he was trying to save our blankets, he left my dictionaries behind. What could I say? They were gone. YienTse thought we must get to Yuenyang by the next morning. If any later, we could get in line of fire of the enemy planes again. Liang Gao was afraid that it would be difficult to walk at night, so YienTse came up with the idea that we should count the train carriages as we walked along the tracks because it will keep us in the direction we want to go, it will keep us together, and it will keep us awake. We agreed that it was a good idea and walked for about two hours. The sky was absolutely black—no moon, not even any stars. After some time, we could see some lights in the distance and could make out a small village not too far away. RenPu suggested that we should be there and get something to eat. Liang Gao said that it would be good if there was a hotel!

When we arrived in the little village, we saw oil lamplights in the distance and felt relaxed as help may be at hand. We came to what looked like a small eating house or noodle shop. There was a man sitting at the front door.

We asked him, "Do you have anything to eat?"

"Yes, fresh noodles."

RenPu said, "Enough for four people?"

"It will be two and a half yuan for four." RenPu was immediately angry and took up a large stick, ready to strike the man to his face. (In today's reckoning, it would be $75.)

"Chiao ju-gan."(outrageous) No wonder RenPu was furious. It was an unreasonable price.

YienTse quickly said, "All right, do you have any scallions, ginger, and salt?"

185

The noodle shopkeeper nodded sullenly.

"All right, please boil some water."

"Then I will have to add another fifty fen."

YienTse agreed and paid the man immediately. RenPu looked on incredulously at the patience and lack of anger on YienTse's demeanor.

"Is there a hotel or inn around here?" YienTse asked.

The man said, "No, there is none such here. Normally, on market days, people come here in the morning, do their shopping and business, and leave before it gets dark. There is no need for any hotels. If you want to rest, I can loan you a grass mat, and you can lie down here."

YienTse thanked him. Then the man dragged a piece of green mat and put it in front of us. RenPu unrolled it and saw that it was covered with chicken shit. His face became red, and we could see his fury rising again.

Quickly, YienTse stopped him and asked the man, "Do you have any dry hay?"

This time the man began to feel that he had overstepped his bad behavior. "Yes, yes, yes," he said and went to the back of his house and brought a large bundle of dry hay.

RenPu spread the hay on the chicken shit mat. Then we all squeezed on the hay together, covered ourselves with our wool blankets, and fell fast asleep immediately.

The sky had just lightened when YienTse woke everyone. We picked up our blankets without saying anything to our less-than-friendly host and started, at once, to walk toward Yuehyang. After one *li*, we saw a man carrying a briefcase sitting by the side of the railway tracks; and as we came closer, we saw that he was our regiment doctor.

He was delighted to see us and said, "Now everything will be all right. I will survive."

I asked him, "Why are you talking like this?"

He said that he had walked all the way from HungPu and only now caught up with us. He had thought everyone had died.

"If I had not met you, if the Japanese devils did not kill me, then the wild dogs would have eaten me."

I said, "That would not happen. The Japanese devils do not come here, and there are no wild dogs or wolves here. You are too tired. Come, let us all walk together."

I felt my head was swimming, and I had a throbbing headache. Everything seemed blurred and dizzy. I thought that I had not slept well.

The doctor looked at me and said, "ChiPei does not look well. He is flushed and weak and unsteady on his feet."

He took my temperature and was very surprised and called to YienTse, "Secretary Chief, ChiPei has a temperature of over one hundred- and four-degrees Fahrenheit. We must find a place and let him rest." YienTse was worried and asked RenPu to go ahead, each person carrying me along between them. We walked toward a house where a white-haired man was standing at the door, looking out with a far-off look in his eyes.

"What's the matter? What are you carrying that young soldier? Do you need help?" he shouted from his house.

YienTse said, "He has a high fever. Please let us rest here for a while."

"Very well," said the old man and asked his son to remove the door planks and put them on two long benches to make a platform makeshift bed in the central living room.

They laid me on this. Then he asked his daughter-in-law to immediately boil some water and make some rice gruel—*xifan*. We were deeply grateful and asked them not to take so much trouble.

The old man then said to us, "Do not be so polite. For the sake of our country and people, you do not bother about your own comfort and safety. This kind of sacrifice I can only admire and kowtow to you all. The year before last, my own son had joined up, and I have not seen him since. Please, I request you to find out where he is."

Now we realized why he was standing outside his door, looking out when we arrived. He was looking out for his soldier son. "I had received a letter from him many months ago that he was in the Eighty-fourth Division, but since then, I have heard nothing. I had written several letters to his children and still got no answer."

YienTse said, "Old Uncle, rest assured, you have his division number. We will try our best to find out for you."

Then his daughter-in-law told us that the food was on the table. YienTse was embarrassed and said thankfully, "That xifan was enough. How could you ask us to go and eat more dinner? We did not want to give you so much trouble."

The old man said, "You are not disturbing us. You are all young and healthy. That little xifan is definitely not enough. Also, you must continue your journey. Who knows how long you will be traveling? So please eat enough and nourish your strength. It is our privilege to help in any little way that we can."

YienTse looked at the dining table all laden with rice, savory dishes, and a large bowl of chicken soup.

"Aya, come and see what this old uncle and his daughter-in-law has done for us. It is indeed a gift we can neither decline nor accept without deep gratitude."

The daughter-in-law said, "Please start. This chicken is our best egg-laying hen. Old Father said that you all are saving our country and are our heroes. He insisted that I must make this soup, that only this act will prove to himself his gratitude to you all." These few words made even our tough soldier RenPu drop tears down his often-red and angry face. (This was a feast that would revisit me time and time again in the future, especially when I was, decades later during the early 1960s, interned in the camp in India).

Then I thought about our recent experience with the chicken-shit man. What a difference. I often remembered the saying that 'WoXiang people are very sincere and kind.' We rested until the middle of the night, then thanked the old man, and said that we had better be on our way.

YienTse tried to give him five yuan to make up for the many expenses he had incurred. The old man adamantly refused to accept it and even said, "If you cannot depend upon this village old man, then I have nothing to say."

We thanked him profusely again and promised to find out what had happened and where his son might be. We told him to take care of himself, and when peace returns, we would try to come and visit him.

The old man sadly replied with a deep sigh, "Ah, you all take care of our country."

I turned my head as we walked away and caught the old man's eye. He was just wiping away the tears. I was deeply moved and said to YienTse, "China is truly a large country. Within such a small distance, people are so different. The difference between this old grandfather and that chicken-shit noodle fellow cannot be measured."

To which YienTse replied, "This is the reason why the Jap devils can never beat us. Now let us not talk of this anymore. How are you feeling. Has your temperature dropped?"

I felt a lot lighter, but my head was still hurting. The doctor took my temperature again. It was still 104 degrees Fahrenheit, so he gave me another injection. We could hear some continuous gunfire in the distance, at which point the doctor threw down his bag and ran forward, shouting, "The enemy is here. Quickly, run, run, run."

I sighed and smiled. "This doctor is cowardly, but he is a good man. He himself ran away, but he left us his doctor's bag. Ha-ha."

"Ha, the guy is good, but he is a useless person [Chinese euphemism for "one who has absolutely no redeeming features"]. His throwing his medical bag had to be a reason. He wanted us to carry it for him, so he could run faster!" When we arrived at Chang Sa, should we return it to him? In doing so, he not only did not have to carry it but also appear to be 'bighearted' by leaving it with us." We all laughed heartily. Doc was cunning to be able to figure out all this. We never did find him, so we left his bag in the nearest hospital.

None of us had been to Yuenyang, but I had remembered it from the Tang dynasty poet DuFu, who had written a poem called "Climbing

Yuehyang Lou [mansion]." I had always imagined how he had described the TungTien *Hu* (lake) covered by mist so heavy that one could not see the distant shore; or from the roof of the Yuehyang *Lou* (tower), one could see the varied and beautiful scenery down below like a wonderful dream. Now we had arrived in Yuehyang, I saw only a broken city—fallen roof tiles and collapsed walls were strewn all over. I wondered and feared the Yuehyang Lou too must have collapsed. We were told that the Japs had bombed the town last night and left nothing standing. Not a 'patch of good skin was left.' We were depressed by the awful destruction but suddenly remembered the train we were supposed to catch, so we rushed to the station just as the train was about to leave, we found our seats just in time. On the train, we spoke about the Yuehyang Lou and the devastation we had just witnessed. That afternoon, we arrived in Changsa. YienTse suggested that we rest for an afternoon before checking into our regiment. We booked into a hotel, four people in two rooms. Then we went to a restaurant to have a proper meal. I was amazed by the length of the chopsticks and the large size of the spoons and bowls and imagined that the people must be proportionately big, strong, and big eaters. We also spoke about our current problems. YienTse, RenPu, and JingGao said we should follow whatever our division was doing. I agreed, but I had to find out whether my household was in Nanchang because if everyone went to Sichuan, then what about my family? They will not be able to leave by themselves. I must go to Nanchang to fetch them to come with us. YienTse agreed.

After reporting to our division, I went to the principal to get permission to go to Nanchang to fetch my family. Permission was granted, but I had to return within a week; otherwise, I would be dismissed. Immediately, I prepared my luggage and said good-bye to my traveling companions of these past few weeks. At the station, I discovered that there were two trains: one went to the battlefront and the other to Nanchang. I was most surprised that all the women and children were climbing onto the train that was going to the front. I asked the stationmaster whether there was some mistake. Were we trying to fool the Jap devils?

He said, rather annoyed, "The train on the right is going to the front. The left is going to Nanchang. You did hear wrong. We are not trying to fool the devils."

So I thought those women I had spoken to were mistaken. I quickly went toward a lady with three children in tow and asked, "Where are you going?"

"To Nanchang to look for my husband."

Then I heard a shout, "You are wrong. The Nanchang train is on the left. The one on the right is going to the battlefront!"

She heard and started to cry, "Aya, aye, *o de ma* [oh my mother]! Please, young soldier, I beg of you. Do a good deed, I still have luggage and relatives on the wrong train. Please tell them to come over here."

I quickly told them that the Nanchang train was on the left, *not* on the right. All those people who heard rushed to the left and those already on the wrong train started to panic and shout and scream and cry. But the soldiers refused to let them onto the correct train.

I explained to the soldier, "They are Nanchang soldiers' families. Please help them onto the train." The soldier saw my badge—red edge, blue writing, denoting that I worked for the San Ch'ing Tuan—and gave way. I ordered everyone to change trains.

Alas, in the confusion, I lost my own seat and ended up sitting in the coal car, but at least sitting anywhere was better than standing all the way. Every time a shovelful of coal was used, my seat lowered a bit. By the time we came to Jiangxi, I was not much higher than those seated on the regular benches. While I was contemplating on my unusual seat, I heard sounds of planes. I shouted to the engine driver, who immediately stopped the train and told everyone to get out and run and hide amid the trees and wheat fields. Not five minutes later, the loud sounds of planes were heard overhead. There must have been thirty or so over us. I lay motionless in the wheat fields behind a very fat man lying on his stomach who was squirming all the time. I could not tell whether he was ill or something. I told him to stop wriggling or he would alert the planes and we would all be shot, but he would not stop. This made me mad, so I strongly slapped his bottom. This made him stop. When the bomb alert had stopped, he stood up, and I thought he was going to fight with me; but he apologized, saying that he just could not stop wriggling until I slapped him. He happened to be the policeman accompanying the train.

When everyone had re-boarded the train, he announced that I was a man with unusually acute hearing, saying that I had heard the enemy planes long before anyone did and, furthermore, had told the engine driver to stop the train and gave all of us time to escape and hide.

"We should all thank him," he shouted, pointing at me.

Everyone thanked me. Ever after, I was nicknamed Big Ears by my fellow soldiers because of my acute hearing.

The next evening, we arrived in Nanchang.

Shing Yin (Temporary/Moveable) Office

I followed Hsu's directions and soon arrived at her place. She lived behind the Shing Yin office. At first, I did not know what kind of office it was; but later, I realized that it was Chiang KaiShek's office. There was an assistant in charge of miscellaneous things, there was a cook, and various "janitor types." The assistant in charge was named Tseng, but Hsu called him Uncle Tseng, and the other one was Uncle Yang. She introduced me to them and told me that she had told her younger brother, Tong, to look out for me at the station. But there was bad news. Changsha was in flames. A deliberate burning had been ordered from above, the 'scorched earth,' - nothing was to be left for the Japs when they arrived.

"Before I saw you, I was terribly worried. It was if my heart was on fire," she said, which made me feel rather pleased but also sad that she had to worry so. It had been a very long time since we were together. This was almost like a new meeting. My heart was also on fire but for a different reason. I could feel the blood rush to my face and looked away. Hsu was similarly affected and also turned away. Damn Confucius.

Hsu then said when we had collected ourselves, "Now I am worried about Tong. He is in the Thirteenth Division and a true soldier. I hope he does not jump into the fire to look for people." Suddenly, someone announced, "How could I be so stupid as to jump into a flame to look for anyone?" Hsu spun around and was elated to see her handsome younger brother, Tong.

"Good, good, I will make lion's head tonight to welcome you both."

"If you are going to make that, then make an extra one for me." Hsu's father had also arrived. Chow Tong and I helped Hsu make the mince out of the fresh pork we had just bought. At night, we made a large bowl of lion's head. There were at least eight big ones. We exchanged four of them for four vegetable dishes with Juen Tsang.

ChowBaba and I discussed as to whether I should return to Changsha.

"Sun Ch'ing Tuan is already in retreat, so there is no reason to return to Changsha, which is destroyed anyway, so you can remain here for the time being.

"ChowTong was already sent to Wong's division to Wei SceeLiang, a protective Third Division. Tong had just graduated and was fortunate to obtain such a good position. The way I saw it was that San Ch'ing Tuan was also being disbanded, the few leaders have already been transferred, and there was no need for to go to Changsha. Just stay here for the time being. Something will turn up. Today it is up to you. You can find work anywhere you want," ChowBaba said.

Then I told my father-in-law, "When I was at Tsung Ho Pu, enemy planes attacked us, and at that time, I had thought that I would have lost my life, not realizing that I may yet see Changsha. I had planned to take Hsu first to Changsha then onto to Chungking because the principal had told me that we would retreat to Jerjiang near Chungking. I also thought that when we arrived there, I would go and visit my mother. My family, since moving from Sikhang to Chengdu, had never really settled down. After our move, my father had to return to the border area to continue his work. I never saw him again. My mother was an old-fashioned lady *goo-koo lin-ding*, (alone and without help), had she not taken along my elder sister, I do not know how she would have survived. The year I graduated from Nanjing University, she had sent me twenty yuan, which she must have been saving from her grocery money. They must have been scrimping and saving every fen. I could not spend that money, so I put it in a red paper packet. Years later, I bought some renshen in Chengdu for my mother."

Lan Cheng Town's One Thousand Spirit Meeting Place (Club)

The Shing Yin Bureau, or moveable office, was near the city wall; and at the base of this wall, some people had stacked some firewood to build a makeshift fireplace. On top of this, they put a very large iron pot. They then went to neighboring restaurants to collect all the leftovers and put everything in this large pot. For the cost of five brass coins, anyone and everyone could buy a substantial bowl hot and probably tasty meal. I saw that there were always a large number of people gathered there, eating and drinking.

One day I walked up to the iron pot minder and asked, "How much for a bowl?"

"Five brass coins."

"Hao, give me a bowl," I said. I took the steaming bowl of *tsa shui* (meaning hodgepodge, the original *chopsuey* of Chinese restaurants outside China) and was just about to eat it when someone held my hand from behind. I turned around and saw that he was my 'boss.'

He let me go and said, "My dear young department head, did you look at the people who come to eat here? Have you forgotten your station, your position, and your uniform? If the uniform inspector found you here, you will be in serious trouble."

"I only wanted to taste what they were making," I said sheepishly. So, I returned the bowl of *chopsuey* to the proprietor, who poured it back into the kettle. He was about to return the five brass coins, but I told him to keep them.

"Your soup must be delicious, and you are helping the poor afford a good hot and nourishing meal. You are doing a good thing."

The 'boss man' said, "You are indeed a good man, but you are no soldier. A soldier must be able to pick up and do anything and yet, when the time comes, be able to put down what he had."

I thought to myself, *Is this not what I just did?* I said, "Old Uncle, I agree."

We left, and then I told him about the incident of my saving the dictionary from the university library until it was burned in the train carriage and how I had to let go and forget about that.

"You are indeed one who escaped death to come here. No wonder your father-in-law said that your life is big, but I think you are also very lucky. You have such good friends to help you in your difficulties."

"Yes," I said, "there was a friend called Wu YiehTse who would die for me and I for him if needed. He was supposed to be Li JiaJao's secretary, but he did not accept the job because he would rather become San Ming Tuan's chief secretary as he thought he would be more useful for the country here. He did not care about the reduction in rank and salary." Boss man was surprised. I said, "Yes, that was his choice."

Kue YinChin, another friend of mine, said that during the time of war, every individual's responsibility, especially the soldiers, should help the country's difficulties. Kue himself should have been a major general, but he had refused the promotion in order to be with his regiment. I was San TsenQi's (Henang) Middle School professor and training officer, but when I arrived at San Ming Tuan, I had to be the teacher because they needed one. I was also paid a lower salary. So, we all do our little sacrifices for our country. But Cheng Shu did not agree because he said that doing little things like this for our country does not really do that much. He felt that the separation and stratification would encourage people to be more ambitious and achieve higher ranks and salaries and do bigger and greater things. He continued, "You three San Ming Tuan boys, how many people do you think can really understand the sacrifices you are talking about? I believe that one should work according to his ability and not be concerned about what others think."

We still wanted to argue and debate, but we had arrived at the office. Yang SuSu came out, saying, "Where did you go? We are waiting for you to eat."

Cheng SuSu laughingly said, "We went to the One Thousand Flavor Meeting Place."

"Is that the city-wall place where all the leftovers from all the city restaurants are taken? Soups, dishes, vegetables, meats—everything—all put into a gigantic iron kettle and reboiled and then resold to all those paupers and homeless, the big pot dish! Could eat their heart's content for only five coppers?"

"Right," Cheng Susu said, nodding.

Yang SuSu then turned to me and said, "Do you really want to eat all those dirty things? You should never eat those things. Do you know that it's the leftovers from one thousand or more people? How can you even think about trying that?"

I said, "I listened to Cheng SuSu. I did not eat it, but I admired that One Thousand Flavor's proprietor because he boiled all those leftovers and made them safe so that even the poorest of the poor can afford a hot, tasty and healthy meal to their heart's content, so their entire bodies are warmed and comforted. Without much consideration, he has done a great act of kindness. Nowadays, such a kind and thoughtful man is rare."

The others listened quietly and nodded.

Hsu's Father Is Promoted to Be the Third General in Charge of Matériel

Chow-BaBa told me that he had been promoted to be the chargé d'affaires of the Third Matériel Division and must immediately take up the position in Chiangxi Yuanjin. I asked him whether Yuanjin was the Communists' "old nest."

"Yes," he replied, "but the Communists agreed that during the war they will not give us any trouble—that the Communists and Nationalists should band together and fight our common enemy: the Japanese. Now I must tell you, there are a few vacancies that must be filled: division head, secretary, and transportation officers. If needed, we can add one or two more people, such as the assistant division head, assistant, chief clerk, and clerks of different departments, etc. You know what I mean. See to it." General Chow (Hsu's father) wanted me to be the SaoXio TsanMo in the Tsan Ma, whose head was a man called Mr. Liu and who had been introduced to me by General Wang. Mr. Liu had graduated from the fourth class of Huang Pu School, and he was busy at the front and could only join us a month later. So I was the temporary division head. I asked Chow-Baba, "The most important work is the dispatch of matériele. What transportation do we have?"

"You must ask the chief of the Transportation Department, a friend of mine." That man had lived in Juehjing for half a year, and he already had his transportation office prepared and even found four or five dormitory-style accommodation for us. My dormitory was in a very famous building and was only one about one hundred steps from my office. I was glad Hsu and I could move into it right away. The second daughter-in-law of the owner of the property took care of the house. She prepared breakfast for the farmers very early in the morning, and then at 3:00 p.m., she sent another meal to them in the fields. They had many helpers, so running hither and thither were all her responsibilities. Though she was very busy, she was never confused or frustrated and was able to take care of everything. Hsu wanted to cook too so that she could take care of her father and me personally, so she asked the landlady if she could find a helper for her.

The next day she brought a strong village girl to help us. She introduced me to her as Tsung Kuang and Hsu as Tsung Kuang's wife.

The girl immediately said, "'Tsung Kuang's wife' is very awkward. I shall just call her Tsung KuangTai, all right?" I laughed, which seemed to upset the girl, who grumbled, "What is there to laugh about? Did I speak wrong?"

Hsu said, "No, no, you are right. 'Tsung Kuang's wife' does sound awkward. Just call me Tsung KuangTai.

"So what do you want me to do?" she asked.

"There are a few pieces of dirty clothes. Take them to the river and wash them."

"I can do that. I used to wash clothes for those leaders, sometimes I washed a hundred pieces. Those men were very nice. They used to joke with me, and we used to eat and drink tea together."

When I heard her say this, I was surprised. She thought we were soldiers and 'leaders.' We were not like her previous employers. We would not joke with her.

I quietly asked the landlady, "Is she deliberately criticizing us?"

The landlady said, "Absolutely not. She is an ingénue villager and cannot read or write. But she did wash clothes for the Communist soldiers when they lived here. You know that the Communists liked to show the poor villagers a little kindness, make them feel that they were one of them. We are ignorant and unschooled. We do not understand anything, but I think if she stayed with you for a short while, she will be very grateful. During these few days, I have already found that you are kind and straightforward. Please hire her. Even though she is rather slow, she is an honest and good person. She can tell the difference between good and bad. I am trying to help her. Thank you."

Chapter 8

TRANSFERRED TO ANHWEI DISTRICT

Hsu's father, Chow-Baba, was promoted yet again to head the Department of Transportation of the Third Matériel Division because his own supervisor, General Gu ChowTung, had himself been promoted to be the Third Staff Office's head of department. The previous head of this Department of Transportation was a friend of Chow-Baba's, and he was able to find us a place to stay, which was owned by a garment factory. However, the factory's looms worked all night, and it was difficult to get a good night's sleep, especially now that Hsu was pregnant. Fortunately, her gynecologist, Dr. TaiYi, had a relative who had a large flat in town, which was for rent. We found a maid with a husband in the army and who had escaped from Juchiang. Chow-Baba also sent us a cadet to help around the apartment. Every day, we had to work until 9:00 p.m., so I had to call out to the guard at the city gate to open the gates for me. This was a time of war, so we could not be too particular about our safety. One day, at about 3:00 p.m., Hsu asked me to go take a walk with her. I asked, "Where are we going?"

Hsu said secretively, "You will know when we arrive."

I cleared my desk and accompanied her out, going along the road that led outside the city gates. After about one li, several cars came toward the town.

Hsu shouted excitedly, "Daole, daole," (arrived, arrived)

Tears poured down her face. I had no idea what was happening until the car stopped in front of us. Hsu rushed to the car and shouted, "Mma, Mma."

I then realized that Lao TaiTai plus Hsu's youngest brother, Chow-Fu; her second sister, Chow-Pu; the youngest sister, Chow-Chi; and Hsu-Fu's concubine had all come. Even ChowTong—the eldest brother, Hsu number two sibling—had come from Chungxi to Dingtong to visit. It was a large family reunion. No wonder Hsu deliberately kept everything such a secret. Normally, Lao TaiTai stayed at home; but this time she had to make the trip from Yangchow to SanLiAn on the north bank of the Yangtse River to Anhwei on the south bank. No one could understand how she made the journey with her small bound feet and difficulties of walking even a few steps, not to mention that we were surrounded by Japanese enemies, plus 'one thousand mountains and ten thousand oceans'—it was no small achievement for Lao TaiTai. Then she pointed to a girl sitting in the back of the car. "Do you know who she is?" I looked closely and saw that she was the Yao family's littlest sister. "Aya, Xiao Tse, you have come too?" "Yes, I have also come. Do you welcome me?"

I replied, overjoyed, "Of course, welcome, welcome, twenty thousand welcomes."

Then Lao TaiTai said, "There is another, Liu YaoJu, Hsu's Nantung friend. Without him, we would not have made it."

I said, "Liu YaoJu, the one from Nantung College?"

"He is the one," said the little girl.

"How did you meet him?"

"We met at SaGo. There, one day, a person called Meow at the Nantung Hospital Medical College. I forgot his name."

"Is it Leow KaiSu?" I asked.

The girl said, "Yes, yes, yes, I asked Uncle Leow if she knew Chow Hsu."

He said, "She is my colleague. How can I not know?"

Then I asked him, "Do you know a LiuLei?" and he said that she was a nurse and was also Liu YaoJu's younger sister. "I hear he is a doctor here. Can anyone tell him that his sister is here?" Liao replied that it would be difficult. "We are scattered to numerous places, and Nantung has been occupied by the Japanese devils we cannot even ask. I knew Liu YaoJu from YuTao, where several of my fellow students worked at the hospital. Maybe we can find out from one of them if there is any news of Liu

YaoJu. This may not be possible, but we can hope. I felt as if I were sitting on pins and needles at home. Luckily, my father, Yao, and Chow BeiBei were posted together, so I got out. If I had been alone, I would not have dared. Later, I heard that Chow Bei-mu and her children were traveling to AnWei, so I asked if I could come along with them. We had heard that Liu YaoJu had been seen in Yu GaoXien and that he too was coming to HweiZhou, so maybe he could come with us too." It was not easy to keep track of what she was so excitedly reporting.

I turned to Hsu. "This was a big organizational job to keep so secret."

Hsu immediately apologized, "This is a good event but a very secret one. Baba had told me not to tell anyone and just to say that he was taking Chu BongYieh and Lou XienMing, two adjutants, to receive someone important!"

Hsu continued, "Everyone has arrived safely, so now the secret is out. Today we rest well, and tomorrow, we will prepare a large welcome feast. They all came like a gust of wind." Hsu also invited another old friend to celebrate our gathering. This is the first time I had seen the entire Chow family—a big family reunion.

Anhwei—Taipin

There were soldiers on either side of the Yangtze River. The Japanese devils used airplanes to bomb us, they used guns on the ground to kills us, and they put diseased rats into our wells to poison us. My Hsu had contracted plague herself because she had come in contact with a sick rat in the hospital where she was working. Had it not been that she was a valued nurse and was able to get treated with sulfur guanidine, I would have lost her. She was one of the very rare people who actually survived the Black Plague. At that time, the Americans assisted us with ammunitions while the USSR gave us several sixty-pounders. I personally accompanied their shipment to the headquarters of General Wong JingJue. He was very happy see me deliver them and said to me, "Old Little Brother, you came just in time. The enemy wants to defeat Taiping. Now I can show them my true color!"

He then personally located and aimed the bombs at the Japanese devils on the banks of the Yangtze then ordered, "FIRE!"

Lightning flashed followed by two thunderous roars. On the shore, there were about one hundred Japanese, and a fast boat was tied to the docks. After the two bombs found their targets, there were ashes and dirt all over the place. The Japanese on the banks were annihilated. General Wong jumped up and down with glee. I learned that he had studied to be a bombardier in war college, and now he wanted me to become a bombardier. He had successfully done his task. He told me to ship the rest of the bombs back to HQ and that he would tell the head that he was keeping me. I was most amazed and rendered speechless.

I returned and told Du BeiBei, who said, "You better do as he commanded." His tone was short. "Go. Get going quickly."

After leaving Huang Shan, we arrived near TongXi. On the road, there was a large red banner across the road. These words were brushed across the cloth: "Those who retreat from the front will be executed."

I saw many wounded soldiers lying about the road, groaning and complaining and accusing any passersby who did not and could not help, but dared not cross the banner. I did not know what all this was about and told the driver to continue ahead. As we approached the banner, an armed soldier stopped us.

I asked, "Why are you stopping us?"

"Can you not read?" he said, pointing at the banner.

"Of course, I can read, but I am shipping matériele."

A short and plump soldier came up to us to see what was going on. I recognized him at once. He was Tang SceTsen. I had met him in HangChow and again in DingTang and even had him over to dinner once. He was the head of the Twenty-third Division in Sichuan and the third assistant head.

I called out, "Tan TsenKuan."

He heard me, turned, and looked at me. "Aya, little brother, how come it is you? Where did you come from?"

I replied, "Yes, it's me. Last night, I shipped these bombs to General Wong JuRen, two of which he set off and successfully and wiped the Japanese on the shores, then happily ordered me to ship the rest of the bombs back. He said that he would report to you, so you must already know about all this."

"Yes, I do." Then he ordered the armed guard to stand down, and turning to me, he said, "Wong JuRen reports to HQ, not to me. Little brother, fortunately, you can mix among those at HQ. Otherwise, we Sichuanese could only *da dwe dwe* [gather together] only in Sichuan." Tang Tsen Kuan considered me to be a Sichuanese also because I was from Sikhang, on the border of Sichuan. He asked me whether I would be staying in TongXi. I told him that my orders were to return to DingTang.

I continued, "If there were no other business, I would continue to TongXi, but I must take these bombs back to HQ." Then I turned to those wounded soldiers on the road. "Those wounded soldiers lying on the side of the road all came from the front. They were fighting for our country and were unafraid to die for it. Today some have lost their legs, some their arms, and now they are thrown by the roadside, and no one seemed to care. I spoke to some of them and found that they were all from Sichuan, many even from your division."

When TungLao heard that those wounded were all Sichuan soldiers, he at once shouted angrily to the guards, "Why don't you send them to the hospital instead of letting them to wallow in this mud on the road? What are you waiting for?" Then he started to round up the wounded and arranged transportation for them.

I said to Tung SceKuan and saluted him. "I must leave. I'm afraid if it gets too late, I might encounter another bombing from the devils."

"Hau, hau [Okay, okay]." Then using a Sichuan native dialect, he said, "You are okay."

Deep-Ditch *(Shen-Khen)* Dates

At first, our office was in the heart of the city, but the Japanese were always bombing the city; so we moved to a fifty-families village called

DingTang, which was situated along a small river about fifteen to twenty *li* from town. There was a single bridge across this river and was the only way to Anhwei. We were posted there for about a year; during this time, the small river ranged from a large-raging one to a small stream. Once, a fellow soldier sent me a box of sweet dates. I discovered from the label on the box that it was from Tianjing, which is very far away, near Beijing.

"Where did you get this?" I asked the soldier.

"Can't you see on the box that it is from Tianjing?" he answered tartly.

"So you went to Tianjing recently?" I persisted.

"Are you mad? Did I go to Tianjing? Phoo, even if this was peacetime, I would not go there," he replied impatiently.

"Then where did you get this box of Tianjing dates?" I insisted.

"Far away near the horizon or right in front of your eyes. I bought it nearby."

"You are talking nonsense. In this little place, except for the street-side noodle shop, there is not even a shop selling odds and ends. How can there be any Tianjing dates?"

"Then you don't understand. This box of Tianjing dates came from your very Deep Ditch. Have you never gone to the *shen-khen* (Deep Ditch)."

"Where is this *shen-khen*? I have no idea. In any case, I don't have the time anyway."

"I don't blame you. You just don't have the time, but there are always opportunities. From the bridge, turn and walk north along the river for five *li*. Then you will be right at the *shen-khen*."

I returned to my quarters to discuss this with Hsu. She was very interested and wanted to go and see. One day we crossed the bridge and walked along the river on the path half an hour. This path became narrower and narrower, and the water became rough and tumbling like many people 'laughing.' We went around the bend in the river, which suddenly opened up again, and revealed a flat field—and in the distance was a house. We walked toward it, and as we neared, we saw that it was a village where the streets were better even than those in HweiChow. We approached a shop and asked if he had any '*shen-khen*' sweet dates. The shopkeeper took out a box, which was exactly like the box that soldier had given me.

I said, "This is TianJing dates?"

"They are TianJing date," he said.

"Then is this from TianJing or from Shen-Khen?"

The shopkeeper was totally confused and did not know what to say. Then a rather old man came out from behind the store. He appeared to be the manager and looked at us and asked, "Mister, what kind of dates do you really want?"

I said, "We want *shen-khen* dates. This shopkeeper gave us Tianjing dates."

The old man smiled and said, "Ah, I understand now. You want the dates with the '*shen-khen*' label, right?"

I said, "Not only the label but also the dates that were grown here."

The old man then said, "I thank you that you are so appreciative of our local *shen-khen* dates. The truth is that the TianJing dates are our *shen-khen* dates. Our manufacturers' association made an agreement with the Tianjing wholesalers that all our dates were to be sold to them. We cannot sell our dates anywhere we like. We are a small village, and though we grow the best dates, we cannot compete with TianJing's large size and *shen* [power], so we are willing and happily sell all our dates through them. We receive a good commission, so we gave up our own name and never call it *shen-khen* dates."

Hsu and I understood the situation and bought several boxes of Tianjing labeled *shen-khen* dates. He wanted to present the box to us free of charge, but I insisted he take the money. Then we said good-bye.

"Aha. PeiKo, (which is what Hsu called me), what a lot of running around just to find the truth about a mere box of dates!" She teased.

I smiled and nodded, "At least we got to the bottom of this mystery."

Once again, after half a lifetime, I have had no opportunity to return neither to HweiChow—where our first child, a little girl, had been born— nor to Shen-khen.

Wong YuenHong and Fong YuenHong

The Third Division in Hweichow wanted to hand over all their military matériele to the Tenth Division and then give the rest to the Communists. Their army leader was named Xing, who claimed that I had been his very good friend for many years. I was surprised at his claim. "Where did we meet?" I asked.

He smiled secretly, "Have you forgotten your good friend from Shanghai? Have you forgotten that you had written something for *Hao Peng You* [*Good Friend*] magazine? I was the chief editor of that magazine." He said, rather pleased with himself, "At the time, I thought your piece was very good and thought that what you had written was accurate. Neither the KungTsan Tang [Communist] nor the KuoMing Tang [Nationalist] were entirely correct and that one should take the middle way. We admired you for your courage to speak out like that." The *Hao Peng You* was a magazine started by some youth in Shanghai; and there, I had met Fang XiTian, who later changed his name to Fang ChangChieng, who had asked me to write pieces for their magazine. "When I went to Wen Zhun, remember, you had asked me to buy for you two large suitcases," continued Xing.

"Yes, I remember now. I had told my batman to bring those cases, and when he brought them, I was taken aback at the size of them. I looked at Hsu who had just given birth to our baby girl not too long ago, and jokingly had said, 'We can easily fit Chin'er into one of them.' Then turning to Xing, I had asked, "How much do I owe you for them?" He did not want to take any money. Just as we were arguing, my batman came and announced that there was a long-distance phone call for me. I went to answer it. It was the HQ's department head, my supervisor Cheng. He said,

"Lao Hsueh, listen carefully, effective immediately: no bullets, no guns, nor drop of petrol will be allowed to be issued without orders from

HQ. If you disobey, mind your head." Normally, we used to joke with each other about 'losing one's head' to some official or other, so I thought he was joking again. I laughed. "No, this is *no* joke. This is the order just arrived from the general from HQ. Thus, this is an urgent phone call." I had just put the phone down and did not even have time to speak to Xing Mo when a soldier with a red card in hand said that a certain Fong YuenHong *Hsiensen* (Mr.) was looking for me. I looked at the name. It looked extremely familiar but could not remember where and when I had met the man. I only said,

"Please ask Mr. Fong to come in." The soldier showed in a man— very tall and big, nattily dressed in his uniform—who then saluted me. I carefully looked at him and returned his salute. He also seemed to be looking at me carefully.

"Are you Hsueh ChiPei?"

"Yes," I replied, puzzled that a he knew my name.

He suddenly approached and embraced me, tears falling down his face. "*TaKe* [Big Brother], is it really you?"

I looked at him again and at last called out loudly, "You are Wong YuenHong. Why are you now called Fong YuenHong?"

He said, "I was always called Fong YuenHong, but later, I was adopted by the Wong family, so I am now Wong YuenHong." YuenHong and I had been in elementary schoolmates in Dawu. I told him of the meeting I had with his father twenty years ago when I read those lines he had posted on the side of his door, about the moon shining on his windowpane from the east. Now after more than twenty years—during all manner of confusion, moving about, and war maneuvers—to meet again like this was surely miraculous. He was moved to tears and related to me how his father had to give him to the Wong family, who had no children of their own, to bring up because his own father was too poor and without a wife to be his mother. I told him simply the difficulties and happenings of these past two decades. He said that he knew about those problems, and today he came to say,

"I have come to tell you that you have been transferred to the Third Political Training Center to not only instruct but also to lead the actual activities of the center. All the work here will be taken over by me, Wong YuenHong." He then formally addressed Xing Mo, "Hsueh ChiPei has been transferred and promoted. I have been sent here to replace him and to take over all his responsibilities. All other business is suspended this afternoon." Xing Mon, when he heard this, was crestfallen. His face turned white, and he forced himself to shake my hand and congratulate me. His hands were cold and trembling. He had thought that he would have replaced me. My entire body felt a real foreboding and realized that some human beings just could not live together. I felt a heavy heart and a lump in my throat.

Capital Moved to ChungKing

It was 1942, and the war was getting desperate. The Japanese Army was moving across China at a rapid pace, but China was a very large country, and people were always ready to retreat from the front. These Chinese were able to '*tsrekoo*' (eat bitter- i.e. suffer) at whatever cost. Nangking had fallen, 'Raped' as the current terminology indicated. But rather than surrender, Chiang KaiShek had moved his capital to ChungKing.

ChungKing, a city deep in the heart of high and steep mountains, most of the time covered in low overhanging clouds and enshrouded in thick impenetrable fog. The Japanese infantry 'devils' would have difficulty negotiating the difficult mountainous terrain, which were also perfect for ambushes. It would also be difficult to send in their flying bombers, or so the High Command thought. But the Japanese bombed relentlessly between 1939 and 1941 in nearly three hundred air raids, and close to twelve hundred bombs, mostly incendiary, were deployed, targeting mainly non-military institutions such as schools, hospitals, factories and residential areas. The Third Political Training Center was also relocated here. I was, therefore, ordered to move to Chungking with my little family. We arrived in the midst of all this destruction, and I have often wondered why we survived. I then remembered the prediction of that old monk, 'he will be protected by the force of his friends.' I now understood. Hsu's brother was now a major in the army, and her father was busy with his battalion; her two younger sisters and baby brother returned to their *lao chia* (old home) in Yangchow with Chow Lao TaiTai, my mother-in-law. So sadly, our family was split apart, with fleeting meetings in the future. I never saw my father-in-law again; and years later, when we were well settled in India, we learned of his execution by the Communist government because of his popularity. Other branches of the family were scattered to FuChieng in South China. Some went to Burma and others to Taiwan. A few of my best friends were executed by the Communists or forced to escape to Taiwan with Chiang Kai-shek's entourage. Such is the nature of war. There is no winner.

Postscript

"I have concentrated mostly on the small, often insignificant and rather personal events of my life rather than the horrors of the war at that time. I felt that there are enough books, records and other people's memoirs, ad infinitum, to add yet another book of remembrances of those demonish years."

Hsueh ChiPei

EPILOGUE

Hsueh ChiPei, my father, died shortly after this in 2003 at the age of eighty-nine, so he was not able to finish his narrative. However, before he died, he had asked to me try to finish it for him. Without his own words this time, I had to rely entirely on my own memories, readings and research. From the time when I can first remember, my father and I had numerous conversations, and he told me many stories, interspersed with the Sung and Tang poems or from ancient historical texts. When I was a young girl, I thought that they were just made-up stories of generals, battles, and 'fun events,' but as I grew older, I realized that they were his life. He had an almost photographic memory. I will try as best as I can to recall them and write them down. Of course, many of the names are now forgotten as they never really meant anything to me at the time, and certainly, I will not be able to quote from any classical Chinese texts, but the events are still rather fresh in my own mind.

This is but the first third of his long life. While his stories and memories are still relatively fresh in my mind, I will continue his passage through Hong Cheng from China to India via the horrors of The Burma (now known as Stilwell) Road. I never let go his ability to joke and laugh through all adversaries – that secret of the rose tint which colors his most outlook on life.

Pu-Chin Hsueh Waide, 2024

Great Falls, Virginia.

www.ingramcontent.com/pod-product-compliance
Lightning Source LLC
Chambersburg PA
CBHW051146120626
46547CB00012B/956